# PRAISES FOR LEADERSHIP ILLUSIONS

"Ken Hartley is a master illusionist, singer/musician, and an inspirational speaker for leadership development. He combines all those extraordinary skills in his enlightening and entertaining book, *Leadership Illusions*. I've traveled around the world with Ken and marveled at his talents, but I'm always more impressed with his humility and servant's heart. Let the truths in this book make you a better leader. Reading this book is just *MAGIC*!"

*– Governor Mike Huckabee,*
*Former Governor of Arkansas and FOX News Contributor*

"Ken has been a leader since I've known him from our high school days and has studied the subject extensively. Although our political convictions differ, we both agree that today, more than ever, leadership is a critical subject. Listen to what he has to say."

*– Van Jones, The Van Jones Show, CNN*

"Ken Hartley is one of the most gifted men I have ever known. He began his leadership role in the area of large church music ministries, a role he has done masterfully. For the last decade, he has become an international instructor in leadership and communication to organizations of all types. His book combines his incredible gifts into a powerful tool that reveals the pitfalls of leadership failure and how to avoid them and overcome them. Using the metaphor of illusion he brings to light leadership strategies that succeed. This is a *must-read* for leaders in every walk of life."

*– Dr. Ron Phillips, Pastor Emeritus, Abba's House*

"*Leadership Illusions* is a must-read primer for anyone stepping into a leadership role. I've never read a book that so clearly and succinctly articulates practical leadership principles, that once implemented, will have an immediate positive impact on how you think, lead and influence. Being an effective leader is a journey. Mistakes and shortcomings will occur. When that happens, learn from someone who has studied leadership extensively and offers practical advice and principles! Have no doubt, these principles, when applied, will fundamentally change a leader's thinking and the direction of their organization."

*– R. C. McDaniel, CAPT, United States Navy*

"Ken Hartley has paid the price, experienced the pain, and has the years of experience to speak to the world about leadership. *Leadership Illusions* will help you avoid the pitfalls that come with the process of becoming a leader. I have seen Ken grow into a powerful leader and mentor over the years and I've learned so much from his journey. I believe you will discover the leader inside of you after reading this."

*– Dr. Ronnie Phillips, Jr.,*
*Lead Pastor, Abba's House, Ronnie Phillips Ministries International*

"As a professional in the financial services industry managing millions of dollars, I found Ken's *Leadership Illusions* book clearly debunks the "one size fits all" leadership approach. Ken appropriately dives into the relevancy of being current with culture and being able to speak the language of those we serve. No matter if you work in manufacturing, professional, or personal service industries, Ken's 21 *Leadership Illusions* are spot on. It's a must-read for anyone serving in leadership."

*– Gary Arblaster, Arblaster Consulting*

### Ken's most important endorsements:

"My dad and I have always shared an interest in self-development, personality assessments, and leadership studies. He helped me cultivate my faith, learn to love all people, and grow my natural skill set. He has embraced the servant leadership role through church ministry and his illusion performances for almost three decades. I am confident his unique and creative insight found in this book will add value to your leadership journey."

*– Megan Markum, daughter*

"I take great pride in being someone who has had the privilege to learn from Ken Hartley's leadership skills for 25 years now. As his daughter, I have been able to watch him lead our family daily, all while being a leader to everyone he knows. Just by the way he lives, he has taught me how to show grace, kindness, and respect in a leadership position, even when times get tough. His daily leadership is a reason I can now be a leader in my field of study!"

*– Brittany Harris, daughter*

"My father has spent countless hours studying the subject of leadership. On top of studying the subject, he has been a pastor for the last 30 years, where he has been required to lead people. He has also led our household and as a result, raised four successful children. With all this experience, he has learned a thing or two about people that are worth hearing."

*– Drew Hartley, son*

"My Dad has spent many hours working on his newest book about leadership. He is a member of the John Maxwell Team and has spoken at multiple large events and has been a pastor for 30+ years. He has had a ton of experiences with people and I hope you can learn from all of those experiences in his newest book!"

*– Trey Hartley, son*

# LEADERSHIP ILLUSIONS

## 21 THINGS PEOPLE BELIEVE ABOUT LEADERSHIP

# THAT ARE NOT TRUE

Jacob,

Be the leader God called you to be. This world _needs_ you!

Blessings!

Ken Hull

John 8:32

**Leadership Illusions**
*–21 Things People Believe about Leadership that Are Not True*
Copyright © 2019 by Ken Hartley

F I R S T   E D I T I O N
*Published in 2019*

**www.HartleyLeadership.com**

ISBN: 978-1-7333818-0-2

Category: Leadership, Mindset, Business

Library of Congress Cataloging-in-Publication Data

Written by: Ken Hartley | Email: ken@hartleyleadership.com
Linkedin: https://www.linkedin.com/in/ken-hartley-b6b331a5/
Facebook: https://www.facebook.com/kenhartleyspeaking/
Twitter: @kenhartley

Cover Design by: Doug Wright

Formatting by: Eli Blyden Sr. | EliTheBookGuy.com

Published & Printed in the United States of America

*For those who know they are leaders,
hope they are leaders, or desire to be a leader—this book
is dedicated to you.
May you find the next steps in your journey here.*

LEADERSHIP ILLUSIONS

# DISCLAIMER

The information contained in this book is strictly for educational purposes. The methods described in the book are the author's personal thoughts, observations, and opinions; they are not intended to be a complete and definitive set of instructions. You, the reader, may discover other methods and solutions that may accomplish the same end results. As a work of non-fiction, the events portrayed in the book are to the best of the author's recollection. While all the events are true, the names of the people, the schools and the educational systems have been eliminated to protect the privacy of all involved. The author does not assume any liability to any party who may interpret any of the recollection of events as a personal slight on their professional status. The author has made every effort to ensure the accuracy of the information in the book was correct at the time of publication.

# TABLE OF CONTENTS

# LEADERSHIP
# ILLUSIONS

## 21 THINGS PEOPLE BELIEVE
## ABOUT LEADERSHIP
# THAT ARE NOT TRUE

### BY KEN HARTLEY

# INTRODUCTION

The new car sat on the stage in the bright lights, elevated on four jack stands about two feet off of the ground. Various items, like a watch and necklace, from the capacity crowd of 3,000 people had been borrowed from some randomly chosen spectators, as well as a piece of paper on which five other audience members had written different things of their choice. All of these items were placed into a small box and then put into the trunk of the car on stage.

Curtains were raised immediately behind the car and to the left and right of it. Before the front curtain was raised, three of my kids took position in front of the car. I asked the curtain to be raised in front of the vehicle for four seconds. The curtain was dropped, and the car (and my kids) disappeared, leaving only the four jack stands remaining. We dropped the remaining curtains to the sides and behind the car, completely clearing the stage and showing that the car had disappeared.

There was a handheld camera focused on the stage that followed us through the back doors of the auditorium and to the front doors of the building. Covering the front exit was a large curtain that dropped as we walked toward it, revealing the car and the kids outside in the parking lot less than ten seconds later. All of the borrowed items were in the trunk of the car.

The audience was blown away and gave me a standing ovation. But that's what I do: I am an illusionist.

I've spent the better part of thirty years doing illusions in front of audiences from ten people to ten thousand and fooled them with both large and small illusions—everything from levitating an audience member to making it snow inside to actually reading their minds. I have had a wonderful time performing illusions all over the world.

One of the things you lose as an illusionist is that sense of "Wow! How did they do that?" Most of the time, you have a very good idea, if not direct knowledge of how most effects are accomplished.

Performing illusions for all of that time also gave me a sense of other illusions hiding in plain sight. Our eyes deceive us nearly every day of our lives. We see something and are just sure it's reality, but the truth is, seeing is *not* believing.

One of my favorite shows on TV is called *The Carbonaro Effect*. Michael Carbonaro is an extremely creative magician who has a hidden-camera show where unsuspecting people are thrust into ridiculous situations using illusions and magic, but they don't seem to be able to recognize that what they're seeing is a magic trick—at least, not until it's revealed to them. The show is hilarious, but it also is revealing.

People often don't recognize the fake or fraudulent until it is pointed out to them. In leadership, it's no different.

Another thing about illusions is that almost everyone wants to know the secret (we'll talk more about this later). But once you know the secret, the "magic" is over. In fact, when most people find out how an illusion is done, the secret seems so apparent that they feel silly for being fooled.

They will make comments like "Oh! Of course! I knew that!" (even though most of the time they had no clue). Some will say, "That's the dumbest thing I've ever seen!" even though just a few moments before they were in shock and amazement. In illusions and magic, the secret is genuinely the magician's best friend. Once it is given away, the magic is ruined. Once you've seen the truth of it, it's nearly impossible to go back.

While I won't be revealing any magicians' secrets in this book, I *will* be pulling back the curtain on some leadership illusions. I'm going to show you exactly where the "smoke and mirrors" are for each one of these and, once the secret is revealed and you see the truth, you won't be able to go back either.

> Our eyes deceive us nearly every day of our lives.
> We see something and are just sure it's reality, but the truth is, seeing is *not* believing.

Real leadership principles have existed since the beginning of time. I won't be telling you anything new. So then why write this book? Because these illusions seem to creep in, and principles, even timeless ones, can be ignored or forgotten. Because you desire more for your life than where you are and what you're doing. Because you want to be a leader ... a real one ... not a fake one.

For us to move past these illusions, we have to expose them to the light of truth and then devise a plan to move forward and not fall back into previous ruts.

That is the purpose of this book you're holding in your hands.

Years ago, I began studying leadership principles. The more I researched and the more observant I became, the more I realized how many illusions existed in the realm of leadership. We have a severe leadership deficit in our world today. People are hungry for true leaders who lead people with direction as well as compassion—leaders who are more interested in *showing* people what to do than merely *telling* them to do it. In corporations, organizations, churches, and yes, governments, leadership seems to be a dying art.

In the United States alone, our Congress—our elected leaders—have basically maintained an approval rating of less than 20 percent for the last decade.[1] What does this say when the people chosen by popular vote (some of them over and over for decades) to lead us have less than 20 percent of the population's confidence?

But the problem is not limited to organizations; it actually begins with individuals. Everyone has dreams and goals of where they want to be. They desperately want to reach those dreams and goals, but they either don't know how, or they don't have a plan to get there.

Most people are not in control of their own lives; they are at the mercy of others who tell them when and how long they have to work. They tell them if and when they can go spend time with their families. Often, when they need to be with their families, permission is denied.

There are two plans for your life. One is your dreams and your goals—that thing you know you've always wanted to do and be. It's been burning in your heart for years. As you read these words, it pops into your mind, and you can feel the fire in your heart begin to ignite.

Unfortunately, there is also another plan in place. That plan for you involves helping someone else fulfill *their* dreams at any cost. It doesn't matter whether it costs you your family, your health, or your goals. They don't care. As long as they increase their bottom line, even at your detriment, they're okay with it.

Is it any wonder that when we're not even leading our own lives as we want, leadership as a whole is a dying art in our society?

Society today is running amok. The lack of leadership has led us to this. As the Bible says, "Where there is no vision, the people perish."[2] We are dying from a lack of vision and a lack of leadership.

Whereas a few decades ago, leaders were "innocent until proven guilty," the opposite seems to be in effect today: People in leadership positions are held under very high scrutiny until they prove themselves.

Dictators with deep insecurities and histories of moral failures and financial mismanagement have led to a lack of respect for people in many leadership positions. It used to be that someone who held a title had a certain degree of respect. Not anymore. Not by a long shot!

Formerly, there was a confidence that leaders had our best interests at heart. Those who didn't were not in leadership positions for long periods of time. Today, there is a general cynicism toward most leadership positions. They are seen as self-serving, egotistical, and occasionally as megalomaniacs.

Speaking as someone who served on the staff in large mega-churches across America, there was a day and age when superstar pastors reigned supreme. What they said was the law (or, forgive me, a religion). They held celebrity status among their congregation and their peers. To question them was ultimately to question God Himself.

But today, everything has shifted.

The day and age of respecting a position are long gone. There is a new model of leadership in this era, and if you don't recognize it and embrace it, you cannot lead people. Some could read those previous paragraphs and conclude we are in a hopeless situation. I would say the opposite.

I'm reminded of the story of two shoe salesmen from a company who flew to an impoverished remote country in Africa. When they landed, they saw all of the natives wearing no shoes. One salesman immediately picked up his cell phone, called the company headquarters, and said, "Fly me back immediately! Nobody here is buying shoes!" The other salesman, upon seeing the natives, picked up his cell phone, called the company, and triumphantly announced, "Send me as many shoes as you can! Nobody here has any! We'll sell thousands of them!"

It's all about perspective!

This leadership deficit isn't a bad thing for you, my friend. It's an excellent opportunity for you to step into your destiny. You can become the leader you were always meant to be! In fact, there has never been a better time than right now to step in and grow into a leadership role. Now is the time for you to increase your leadership skills and become who you've always wanted to be!

I learned a lot of leadership lessons early on. I was thrust into leadership positions in my late teens and I learned a lot more from what I did unbelievably wrong. I screwed up, and I mean a *lot*. I lost people who served with me, and it was all my own fault.

I seemed to be one of those people who wanted people to follow him, but very few actually did. I operated out of insecurity and fear.

But, at the same time, I noticed others who, wherever they were and whatever position they held, seemed to have people follow them naturally. People were drawn to them like magnets. They inspired people to do their best and they empowered people around them to achieve greatness. I thought they were just born that way. I was wrong.

I was forced to come to the inescapable conclusion that I was not a good leader. In fact, I wasn't really a leader at all. It was a harsh reality, but a reality nonetheless. At that point I realized I had a couple of choices: I could retreat into a hole and become like others who had given up on *life or* ... I could learn from my mistakes, study, get better, and press ahead. I chose the latter.

One of my mentors, Dr. John C. Maxwell, taught me that leadership can be learned. And so I studied and I learned. I'm still very much on that journey. You will find, like I did, that the journey never truly ends. The point is, you *can* do it!

Not only *can* you do it, but you also *need* to do it. Our world needs you. Your business needs you. Your organization needs you. Your church needs you. Our government needs you. The point is, none of that matters if you don't learn and recognize these leadership illusions and learn how to overcome them *now*.

I want you to make the same choice I made—right now. Regardless of where you are, you can grow in your leadership skills. In fact, you need to. I don't mean that badly toward you; I mean you have a unique contribution to make, and if you don't become who you are supposed to be, there will be a hole there! The world needs more leaders, and this book can be your first step in a life-changing leadership journey.

I'm going to share a list of twenty-one of the most significant leadership illusions. This list isn't all-inclusive, but it does cover some major ones. It will identify the illusion and give you the truth about each one. I will then provide some action steps for you to grow into your new leadership skills.

Recognizing these illusions will help you spot the truth and avoid them. Applying the truths will change your life and the lives of those you come into contact with. Truth is inevitable. Someone can insist they're wearing a blue shirt, but if you clearly see them wearing a red shirt, you can't deny that. Once you know the truth, you can't escape it. We're about to embark on a truth journey.

If you're ready to change your life and become the leader you were always been meant to be … read on!

> There is a new model of leadership in this era, and if you don't recognize it and embrace it, you cannot lead people.

## What Leadership Looked Like

I remember attending a corporate event in the 1990s. The president of the company stood up to talk to his employees. He spoke for about thirty minutes total, and at least twenty-five of those minutes were spent talking about himself. Honestly, it seemed to be his favorite subject. People in the audience clapped and laughed, but I overheard a very different conversation very near me.

"He's all about himself."

"He doesn't give a rip about us."

On and on these two employees went, talking badly about what they thought about their "leader." Toward the end of his talk, the president mentioned an unpopular decision he had made. There were a few noticeable grunts from the audience. He then leaned forward, pointed his finger at the crowd, and announced, "I may not be right, but I am the president. If you don't like it, you can leave."

He got a standing ovation. I'm not kidding—a standing ovation. Here's the thing, though: The two employees who had been ripping him apart very near me a few moments before were on their feet, smiling and clapping for him a few minutes later.

I'm sure the president looked at the reaction and perceived that everyone was with him, but they weren't. In fact, the more I got to know about this particular organization, the more I realized how dysfunctional it was. People only agreed with him out of fear of losing their jobs.

The president led from his title and from inspiring fear, and honestly, in the 1980s and 1990s, it worked pretty well.

But in the 2000s, things began to shift. There began to be a general lack of trust in leadership. Scandals in large corporations and a barrage of accusations against government officials created a cynicism in our society toward leaders.

It happened in churches too—and I don't just mean moral failures within the church (although there were quite a few of those too). Whereas before there were "superstar" pastors who were iconic in their message deliveries and their larger-than-life personalities who led with iron fists ("Either agree with me or get out!"), congregants started rejecting those dictatorial attitudes and either voting out the leaders or just leaving and finding other places to attend.

The thing is, on the outside most of these organizations seemed healthy. But a closer examination of how things were being run, the satisfaction of those involved in the organizations, and the turnover ratios all revealed quite a different story. Things looked great, but in truth they were nowhere near what people thought.

It was an illusion.

Here's the thing about illusions: When I perform them on stage, people expect to be fooled. They're looking for it. Deep down, they want it. They want that sense of amazement and wonder.

But the real world doesn't work that way.

In the real world, those illusions are right in front of our faces, but we often miss them. We don't even realize we're being fooled.

The previous model of being a dictator—leading from a title or a position, or controlling people through fear and intimidation—is over. Those are failed philosophies that have no future, and organizations that stick to those models are destined for obscurity and eventual extinction. The ones who embrace the reality of what real leadership is will thrive and prosper in the future.

In the real world, those illusions
are right in front of our faces,
but we often miss them.

# CHAPTER 1

# MY LEADERSHIP JOURNEY

From the time I was seven years old, I had an interest that bordered on obsession with the presidents of the United States. Every child has different aspirations growing up, and mine was to be the president. I actually used a school phone (when I was in third grade) to call the White House long distance on the school's dime one time and asked to speak to the president. No, I didn't get to speak to him, and yes, I got in major trouble at school and at home. There are still people in my hometown who remind me of it when I see them.

To me, there was just something amazing about the people who were leading the country, something almost iconic. To this day, I am still very much a student of history and the presidents (although I haven't called the White House since I was in third grade!). I did visit the White House in the mid-1980s and got to go to the Oval Office. I love going to presidential libraries around the country and finding out what motivated the men who held the highest office in the land.

Something can be learned immediately from a study of our presidents. Some of them were great leaders. Others … not so much. And, no, I'm not going to be political here and say the ones I think were great (and weren't). But I will say this: I have learned just as much from studying the bad leaders as I have from the good ones. Sometimes, it's every bit as necessary to know what *not* to do.

I ran for offices in my school and clubs growing up. I won some. I lost some. Looking back now, I was much more interested in getting a position than I was in effecting change. More about that later ...

When I was very young, I moved into a leadership position in a church. I had read some books on leadership and thought I knew a lot about leadership, but truth be told, I was not a leader. I simply had a title. The biggest problem was that I was not aware of that truth until later—*much* later.

I was just eighteen years old when I began leading music in a church. I oversaw twenty-one volunteers every week. I didn't take it seriously because I was in college and was very young and immature.

The church was part-time—very part-time. As I look back today, I see how wonderful and patient those people were with me. Even though our church had about 100 people, we did musical presentations that drew over 800 people from a community of 2,000 people.

After I graduated from college, I left that church and moved to a church averaging 350 people. I stayed there and learned for four more years. From there, I left and moved to Florida to a church of over 9,000 members. I was just twenty-four years old. I would go on to lead other megachurches in various metro areas, one of which had over 13,000 members.

> # I was not a leader.
> # I simply had a title.

I knew what I had done in other places and replicated that process in most of the places I moved to. There was just one problem: After I'd been there for three to four years, I was out of (forgive me) my bag of tricks. I had learned to imitate, but I had never learned to become a leader. I had a program that I bulldozed through and made everyone like it (or at least pretend to).

In the process of my leading these large church ministries, I did some things right. Some of it was sheer dumb luck; some of it, I had learned. But oh my gosh … I did a *ton* of stuff wrong. If there was a way to screw up being an effective leader, I probably did it. The first pastor I ever served with told me, "The good news is you learn from your mistakes. And at the rate you're making mistakes, you'll be a genius in no time."

I led from the weakest position I could. I alienated people. I made them angry at times. I hurt their feelings. I was generally just a bad leader. People would accuse me of being a know-it-all tyrant, and you know what? They were right. Although I got results (lots of growth), that could not justify the casualties. I was just like a surgeon who chose to operate with a chainsaw instead of a scalpel—I accomplished the surgery, but I also massacred a lot of patients!

One of the assets I've had is my work ethic. I would work hard. But even though we were achieving great results and numeric growth (which was plenty of justification to keep a well-paying job in corporate America), I noticed that I didn't truly understand the hearts of the people I was supposedly leading.

I also noticed there were other people on our staff, and even some volunteers in our church, who garnered great respect and loyalty from the people they were leading. It frustrated me because I thought, *I'm putting in way more hours and working harder than these other people! Why are they so loyal to them, and why don't I engender that type of loyalty from my people?!*

I simply did not inspire loyalty in others. So I began to study, and the answer smacked me in the face—very hard and very abruptly.

I worked as hard as I could to grow my music ministry, which was my area of responsibility. I poured everything I had into my job—and everyone saw it. In case you missed the pronouns in those last several sentences, they were "I" and "my." I was working hard at growing my own little kingdom and using other people to do it. That, my friend, does not inspire anyone.

I came to the hard truth that it had all been about me, and I had been using people to further my own agenda, instead of leading them to their God-given destinies.

> I led from the weakest position I could. I was generally just a bad leader.

It was at that point in my life that I intentionally began to study what authentic leadership was. There were (and are) a ton of books on the subject, but my research inevitably led me to the writings and teachings of Dr. John C. Maxwell. Having spoken to millions of people across the world on the subject of leadership, he is considered an expert on the subject. In fact, *Inc.* magazine named him the number-one leadership authority in the world. To top that off, he was also a pastor for many years, so I had an immediate connection with him.

For years, I studied John's books and, through a series of incredible events, I was able to meet John and be mentored by him in the areas of speaking, communication, and leadership. I joined his leadership team in 2017. When I studied his materials, it didn't take me long to face some harsh realities about my own leadership style and skills.

Through learning about leadership, I saw the gaping holes in my leadership skill set. I saw the truth—the undeniable truth. As the Bible says, "The truth shall set you free." (John 8:32.) Knowing the truth, understanding the truth, and applying the truth changed the way I looked at leadership forever, and I believe it will have the same effect on you.

You see, as an illusionist, that feeling of "Oh my gosh, that fooled me!" is a rare and beautiful treat. Very few effects I see on stage, TV, or movies fool me anymore, but I have to confess it does happen occasionally and, when it does, it's a rare and wonderful feeling. But being fooled in the realm of leadership is not fun and, unfortunately, it isn't uncommon either. Even with my years of skills as a professional illusionist, I was badly fooled in this area …

That is, until I learned the truth. Once the secrets of the illusions were exposed, I could no longer view the fake as real anymore. I knew the truth, and it had set me free. I believe the same thing is about to happen to you.

So, in this book, I'm going to break the cardinal rule of illusionists and magicians: I'm going to reveal the secrets. I'm going to tell you exactly the secret that is in play and then explain how to overcome the illusion so that you'll never be fooled again.

The chapters are not long; they're not meant to be. They're intended to expose the lie of the illusion to the truth and to help you overcome the illusion so you'll never fall for it again. At the end of every chapter, I'll also give you some places for personal reflection, where you can write down specific ways you can apply each truth to your life.

So, if you're ready to learn the secrets, let's keep going!

Knowing the truth, understanding the truth, and applying the truth changed the way I looked at leadership forever, and I believe it will have the same effect on you.

# CHAPTER 2

# How Did You Do That?!

If you and I were sitting down together, I could show you some optical illusions online. They look absolutely impossible. And I don't mean camera tricks; I mean legitimate optical illusions that, if you were standing right in front of where that camera was, you'd be fooled. If you'd like to look up one, do a search for "Ames Room," and you'll see one of the many illusions I'm talking about.

You've heard the old saying, "Seeing is believing." As an illusionist, I can tell you, "That's a lie!" In fact, it's the key to many illusionists making a good living! Seeing is *not* believing. Our eyes are lying to us nearly every day of our lives. And yet, we believe them!

A twentieth-century philosopher said, "I love magicians because they're such honest deceivers. They tell you they're going to fool you, and then they do it. But afterward, you still have your watch, your wallet, and your appendix, which is more than I can say for some of my non-magician acquaintances."[3]

Illusionists and magicians are honest deceivers. You, the audience, expect to be fooled and, if the people on stage are doing their job, you are. Other illusions that exist in this world give you no warnings or disclaimers. They simply fool you, and their deceptions can cost you credibility, money, and, ultimately, your destiny in life. That's why it is so important to not fall for the lie and to know the truth.

The number-one response I get as an illusionist is the knee-jerk reaction, "How did you do that?!" When I'm asked that after nearly every show, I politely reply that I cannot tell them the secret. For the illusionist, good secrets are just good business! Let's face it: A magician with no secrets is out of business!

For the leader, believing in illusions has the opposite effect. Believe those illusions are real and you'll be ineffective. Practice them and you'll be out of business.

Every magician who has received instructions on how to do an illusion knows that the process is divided into three sections.

### 1) The Effect

This is what the audience sees and may even believe is happening.

- An audience member was levitated.
- A "ghost" flew around the room.
- The illusionist read our minds.
- A car disappeared.
- The illusionist cut a lady in half.

> Believe those illusions are real and you'll be ineffective. Practice them and you'll be out of business.

But please know, these events are not what is truly happening. I hate to break the news to you, but there is no such thing as real magic. These are all theatrical effects that look a certain way but are really another.

In this section of every chapter, I will tell you what the leadership illusion is. I'll give you an illustration of what it looks like and what other people may actually believe.

Think of this section as the "what." It explains what people see and believe.

### 2) The Secret

Here is where you find out exactly how the illusion works. This is the section many magicians go for first, and then they put the instructions down and never read again. Believe it or not, that happens way more than you think it does.

In this section, you'll know what the smoke and mirrors are hiding and where "the wires" are or where "the girl" is actually "hiding." I will expose the secret of the leadership illusion for you so you can see the truth of it once and for all. This section is the statement of truth. That same truth that sets you free.

Many magicians read the first two parts of the instructions and believe they have something. I believe that is why there are so many bad magicians performing today. An effect and a secret do not a good trick make. Although this is usually the number-one thing a spectator wants to know from a magician, it is often the least important thing they can know. Their curiosity may be satisfied, but that secret doesn't mean they can actually do the illusion.

Although it could change their perception, it won't necessarily change their performance. That takes intentional work.

Think of this section as the "how." It's what is really going on behind the scenes.

### 3) The Presentation

Here is where the real work happens. In this part of the instruction manual, you'll see, step by step, the work of the illusion. It tells you the history of it, the inner workings of it, and how the person who wrote the instructions performs it. But still, that doesn't necessarily make a great illusion.

As I said, lots of magicians read the effect and the secret, and stop there. But not you! You're going to press through into the presentation. That is where the *real* magic happens! This is where you formulate a presentation that is interesting and engaging for your audience. The applications here are only limited by your own creativity.

The real magic of any illusion presentation is in the manner in which it is presented. I've seen a few hack magicians levitate themselves, and I've seen David Copperfield fly. Believe me, there is a difference and, although the principle may be the same, the *presentation* is what makes one person utterly forgettable and the other person one of the greatest illusionists who has ever lived.

In this section, you'll understand why we apply the secret the way we do in a way that will change your life and the lives of the people you work with.

Think of this section as the "why." It's where you will know *why* you'll lead the way you will lead. It's where I'll give you examples of great leaders who have applied the truth—and even some not-so-great leaders who have lived the illusions.

In every chapter, I will list the effect (what people believe they are seeing) and the secret (how the illusion is really accomplished, so you'll know what is really going on). The rest of the chapter will be devoted to giving you examples of the presentation (why people fall for it) and how you can correct your course to never fall into that trap ever again. I'll also give you some questions to answer about yourself. Don't skip past them. Actually, do the work and you'll see a transformation in your thinking and actions and, ultimately, your influence as a leader.

When you read this, I want to encourage you to be *honest*. Look at these illusions and *really* ask yourself if you struggle with that particular illusion. If you really want to be courageous, ask those people who are around you the most if you struggle in this area. Their answers may surprise you. Those can be painful conversations to have, but they could very well be some of the most important conversations you have in your life. That pain can lead you to tremendous and lasting positive transformation.

With each illusion, ask yourself:

- Have I seen this?
- Have I done this?
- What is the *truth*?
- How can I apply it?

There are opportunities in every chapter for you to ask yourself these questions. I encourage you to not just go through and read each chapter without thinking about them; instead, really evaluate and ask yourself if these are things you've either done or experienced. Take some time to reflect. Get a small notebook and write out your journey. You won't recognize yourself after you've taken this journey, and you'll be very gratified by your progress.

Another thing to note: I realize that many of these illusions will not seem profound to you. Some may seem obvious. As a very young illusionist who badly fooled some of my friends with a trick I performed, I made the mistake of telling them how it had been done after they continually begged. Once that secret was revealed, they thought it was the dumbest thing they had ever seen and then proceeded to tell everyone how it had been done. Nice friends, huh? The trick was ruined and I learned a hard lesson.

Don't let the simplicity of the solutions keep you from embracing the full truth of them. These are powerful secrets, and the majority of people are fooled by them. You will know people who've employed these secrets. Some of them, perhaps, are people you've worked with and for. That's the easy part. I would encourage you to go deeper and look for *you*. Keep the focus on the only person you can actually change—yourself.

> ## Don't let the simplicity of the solutions keep you from embracing the full truth of them.

I wouldn't go around sharing these secrets, especially with those in positions of leadership above you. Your job is to correct *yourself*. When you start applying these lessons, people will see the difference in you and want to know what is going on. Then you can begin to explain it to them or, better yet, buy them a copy of this book!

Most illusions, once the secret is revealed, seem obvious, and you kind of kick yourself for being fooled by something so simple. That's why secrets are carefully guarded. Once you see the truth of them, you cannot go back. The same is true of these illusions. You may see the truth, it may seem simple, and you may feel a bit silly for not seeing it before.

In the movie *The Matrix*, Morpheus presents the hero, Neo, with two pills: a red one and a blue one. The red one leads to the truth and freedom. The blue one leads back into the illusion world that

Neo believed to be real. Morpheus says to Neo right before he takes the red pill, "Remember: All I'm offering you is the truth."

The same is true here. All I'm offering you is the truth.

Winston Churchill said, "The truth is incontrovertible. Malice may attack it, ignorance may deride it, but in the end, there it is."

As I said earlier, the hardest part of being an illusionist is that you generally lose the sense of wonder you had as a kid when you saw a performance. You lose the "Oh my gosh! How did they do that?!" That feeling is gone. Once you know these secrets, all that is left is a respect for each person's performance skills. Every now and then, somebody will fool you but, for the most part, you're not fooled anymore. The same thing is about to happen to you with these leadership illusions.

Don't use these secrets as weapons to try to show superiority over someone. That is not what leadership is. Use these truths to increase your own leadership skills and empower others to do the same.

Now it is my time to invite you to come backstage and examine these twenty-one illusions. I'm going to "open some boxes" and show you exactly how they work and how you can avoid them. You'll never be fooled again. So come on back here behind the curtain and let's jump into the first leadership illusion.

Winston Churchill said,
"The truth is incontrovertible.
Malice may attack it, ignorance
may deride it, but in the end,
there it is."

# CHAPTER 3

# THEY ARE A BORN LEADER!

**T**he Effect: Great leaders are just born that way. They have a natural ability they inherited from their ancestors that enables them to be good leaders.

**The Secret:** Leadership is an acquired skill. Some people may have been born with a more dominant personality, but that doesn't make them a good leader. Great leadership is a combination of many skills, all of which can be developed, if a person chooses to do so.

In the 1800s, Europe was in an identity crisis. Emperor Napoleon's conquests across Europe had left it divided and a bit of a mess. Napoleon was ultimately defeated at the Battle of Waterloo in 1815. Among the people who fought against him was a major in the Prussian army, William. William had received his commission to the military as a teenager but, due to his skill as a leader, he was promoted quickly. He had a reputation as a decisive leader who provided his soldiers with a clear understanding of his intent. He knew how to remain in contact with his subordinates.

William earned the Iron Cross for his service in the Battle of Waterloo and was promoted to the rank of captain. He also served as a diplomat for his country. He continued to listen to his subordinates' advice and grew in his leadership skills as a result of it. He was intentional about growing in his leadership abilities and assumed nothing. He knew that true leadership meant being able to influence and lead those in his charge. He eventually rose to the rank of general.

William's older brother, Frederick, became the king of Prussia in 1840. However, in 1860, his brother suffered a massive stroke that eventually cost him his life. William never thought he would be king. Neither did any of his family. But circumstances dictated he would rise to the throne. And rise he did.

Utilizing the leadership skills learned in his military service, he surrounded himself with the smartest, most qualified people he could find. Many of his advisors had opposing political views, but William knew there was value in a diversity of opinions. His most prominent appointment was Otto von Bismarck, whose reforms and policies shaped Europe during the last part of the nineteenth century and led Germany to become one of the four most economically powerful countries in the world.

> Great leadership is a combination of many skills, all of which can be developed.

William I loved the people of his country and championed civil liberties, freedom of consciousness, and other concepts from the Enlightenment. It was William's vision and leadership that in 1871 united the various states into a united country called Germany, of which he became the first emperor, Kaiser Wilhelm I. He reigned as emperor and continued leading Germany into prosperity until 1888, when his son Frederick III took over and reigned for ninety-nine days until he died of throat cancer.

Enter William's grandson: William II.

If anyone had the pedigree to be a leader, it was William II. Born into royalty in William's family but also the favorite grandson of Queen Victoria of England (one of England's greatest monarchs), William had both the look and education of a king. He was known as one of the smartest and most well-informed people of his family. He was also in the military and rarely seen without his military garb during his ascension to power. He had the right pedigree, the right look, the right voice, and the right setting to launch the new empire of Germany into a prosperous twentieth century. If anyone was a "born leader," it was William II.

There were just a few issues. He was deeply insecure. He had a violent temper. He was a bit of an anti-Semitic racist too. He was arrogant, with a know-it-all mentality. He didn't listen to his advisors. In fact, he eliminated those around him who wouldn't agree with him and surrounded himself with people who would simply tell him he was right about everything. Otto von Bismarck (who many still consider the architect of peace in Germany), who had been hired by his grandfather and had become the first chancellor of Germany, was fired by William II almost immediately.

William II micromanaged all of his leaders. He had to be right about everything. He always wanted his own way. In later years, when Bismarck described William II, he said, "He wanted every day to be his birthday."[4]

William II always spoke openly and aggressively about war in order to intimidate and frighten others. What followed in Germany was a series of mistakes and missteps by William II that were blamed on everyone except himself. He attempted to reach out to the French and British by doing an interview for *The Daily Telegraph* in 1908, but his angry outbursts and wild statements only served to alienate them further.

His most notable mistake was when Archduke Franz Ferdinand, a friend of William II, was assassinated in Sarajevo. William II made what was known as a "blank check" declaration and offered to help bring down the ones responsible—and then he left on a cruise. He was out of touch with everyone for the next several weeks. By the time he returned, a series of events had been set into motion that led Germany (and others) into the First World War.

William II would end up abdicating his throne in 1918, and Germany ended up in shambles. Just twenty years later, the downward spiral William II had put Germany on left them susceptible to the control of one of the most evil and vile dictators in history: Adolf Hitler.

How could a country, so healthy and vibrant, spiral in just forty-seven years? Leadership.

If anyone should have been a "born leader," it was William II. So what made the difference in the two Williams? One actively listened and worked on his leadership skills; the other assumed his heritage made him a leader.

Although some people may have a bent toward leadership, real leadership skills are developed through years of study and practical application.

What are some ways you can increase your leadership skills?

1) **Read books on the subject**. I'm glad you're reading this one. This is a good starting point. I would also recommend books by Dr. John C. Maxwell, such as *The 21 Irrefutable Laws of Leadership* and *Developing the Leader Within You 2.0*. John Addison has a great book called *Real Leadership*. I would also recommend that you read biographies of great historical leaders. You can learn a lot from their stories.

2) **Volunteer to lead a volunteer group**. Do you want to know how honed your leadership skills are? Try leading a group

that can choose whether or not they're going to follow you without fear of losing a paycheck. You will quickly discover how effective your leadership skills are.

3) **Get involved in a MasterMind group**. What is that? It's a group of like-minded individuals who are committed to growing themselves by studying a variety of subjects. The group setting creates a synergistic atmosphere where the sum is greater than its parts $(1 + 1 = 3)$. Thinktank groups like these can help you grow exponentially.

4) **Get input from those who work above you and below you**. Ask for honest feedback about your communication and leadership skills and let them know you truly value it. Don't take any criticism as a personal attack and, whatever you do, don't defend yourself. Just listen, take notes, and then thank them. Take it as an opportunity to grow.

5) **Talk to other leaders**. If possible, get a mentor in the area you are looking to grow in the most. Remember, even if a person can't mentor you personally, if they have books, videos, CDs, or podcasts to download, they can still mentor you through their materials, even though you may have never actually met them (*yet*).

6) **Get involved with leadership organizations, both local and national**. These can help you grow immensely, especially if they offer specialized training or classes.

> **Real leadership skills are developed through years of study and practical application.**

Everyone can improve their leadership skills. It takes intentionality and daily progress, but you can do it. Yes, everyone is gifted at something, but gifts without development do little good in the long run. Be intentional about working on your leadership skills every day. If you work on your leadership skills every day, I promise you that you will improve and become a better leader. It just takes time and consistent effort.

> Everyone can improve their
> leadership skills.

# CHAPTER 4

# MY TITLE
# ENTITLES ME TO LEADERSHIP

LEADERSHIP ILLUSION # 2

**T**he **Effect:** A person acquires a title (executive vice president, CEO, facility manager, etc.), and by doing so, they are automatically a leader. The title gives them the right and ability to lead.

**The Secret:** People don't follow titles; they follow leaders. Often, the person without the title is the one actually leading. The person who uses their title to lead attempts to influence from the lowest possible place.

I have lots of friends in the military. I've heard of this scenario over and over: A young, twenty-three-year-old graduates from officer school and enters military life. In the army, they would begin as a second lieutenant. This means they outrank every noncommissioned officer (NCO). Many of the NCOs have been in the army for years and years. Some have over twenty years of experience.

The second lieutenant has a title, and that title gives him authority over the enlisted men, but who do you think the men are more likely to listen to in case of an actual combat situation?

We've seen this play out in times of battle. A platoon is on the field of battle and a new officer arrives who attempts to lead a group of battle-hardened soldiers based solely on what he or she has been told about combat classes. Now, between this officer and a master sergeant who has twenty-plus years of experience and has actually been on the field of combat with this platoon, who do think the soldiers are going to listen to?

According to my military friends, in many instances the NCOs train the new officers who come in. I have a friend who was in command of the largest naval base in the United States. He told me the key to his success in his leadership position was the incredibly efficient work of his NCOs. Their years of experience and their knowledge of the military operations, as well as the enlisted men, made them an invaluable source of wisdom and expertise. He learned to rely on their advice and, because of this, he was very successful in his leadership role, receiving an award from the Navy for his stellar leadership of the base.

This principle holds true, regardless of the title: People follow leaders; people do not follow titles.

Think about these men who all held the same title: President of the United States.

- **Martin Van Buren.** He enjoyed hearing himself make speeches and was known for being a sly politician, but he was an indecisive leader, basically sitting on a financial crisis and doing nothing to alleviate it. He became known as Martin "Van Ruin" by the end of his term.

- **William Henry Harrison.** He gave a 1.45-hour-long speech at his inauguration (it still holds the record for the longest presidential inaugural address ever) in the rain. He caught a cold and died one month later of pneumonia.

- **John Tyler.** He was the first man to become president without being elected (he was William Henry Harrison's vice president). He couldn't get along with his rival party or his own party! In fact, he vetoed legislation proposed by both parties because he disagreed with them. Most of his own cabinet resigned and, because of how he had assumed the presidency, he was dubbed "His Accidency."

- **Zachary Taylor.** When asked where he stood on important issues, he replied, "I don't rightly know." He was a soldier and didn't want to be president at all, but his popularity as a soldier gave him the popular vote. Not only did he not have any political views, but when he was elected president, he had never voted one time in his life. He is credited with killing the Whig political party.

> # People follow leaders; people do not follow titles.

In fact, between 1836 and 1860, our country survived a string of eight lackluster leaders in a row! I could go on and on with other presidents, even in our not-so-distant past, and cite a lack of leadership skill, but you get the picture. The fact that these men held the highest title in the United States in no way, shape, or form made them great leaders.

A title-based leadership assumes two things: 1) Because the bearer has a title, they are a leader, and 2) because they have a title, they are now in charge. Both assumptions are completely false and can be incredibly toxic for any organization.

I was working with a volunteer at a church who desperately wanted me to give him a title for his volunteer position. Don't get me wrong, I'm all about volunteers taking ownership and leading, but he was insistent on getting a title. When I asked him why, he replied, "How in the world am I going to lead if I don't have a title?!"

I had to gently tell him that the title was entirely unnecessary for his leadership role. If he would simply focus on influencing and leading his team, the title would become apparent. That's precisely what he did and, today, he is a paid staff member on a church staff (with a title too)!

If he had started with the title and tried to lead from that position, he would have failed miserably. Instead, he got to know the people he was working with and established relationships with them. Those relationships led him to meet their needs. Meeting their needs led him to a position of influence. That influence made him a leader.

But how can a person who inherits a title become a leader?

1) Acknowledge that the title doesn't give you the right to leadership. If you do this right off the bat, the people you're working with will respect you and give you a chance.

2) Learn the culture you're in. Talk to the people who have been there for a while and find out who the leaders are and who can and cannot be counted on. Who are the "NCOs" in your organization who have put years of blood, sweat, and tears into everything and everyone? Get their input. Let them know you value their opinions and need their help to be effective.

3) Give it time! It takes time to get to know a new organization and a new position. Don't expect this to happen overnight. Real relationships and trust take time.

4) Never use phrases like "I'm the boss" or "My title makes me in charge." Anyone using those type of phrases is clearly not in charge of anything. When phrases like these go flying across a workplace, respect goes out the window, followed closely by influence.

5) You can influence people by adding value to them. Make a list of ways you could add value to the people you're working with and be intentional about implementing that list daily. The more you add value to a person, the more influence you'll have with them.

> Meeting their needs led him to a position of influence. That influence made him a leader.

A title doesn't make you the leader of anything; influence does. I know I've used the word "influence" many times in this chapter. Influence is defined as "The capacity or power of persons or things to be a compelling force or produce effects on the actions, behavior, and opinions of others."[5] Yep. That sounds like leadership to me. But don't just take my word for it. The number-one leadership guru in the world, John Maxwell, says, "Leadership is influence. Nothing more. Nothing less."[6] If you increase your influence, you'll increase your leadership abilities. A title on your door or in front of your name has nothing to do with it; the amount of influence you hold by adding value to others does.

I'll say it one last time for emphasis: Leadership is influence.

A title doesn't make you the leader of anything; influence does.

# CHAPTER 5

# EDUCATION MAKES ME A LEADER

LEADERSHIP ILLUSION # 3

**T**he Effect: "I have a degree in [pick your subject]. Since I have gotten my degree, I am now a leader in my area of expertise."

**The Secret:** A degree entitles you to say you've earned it from wherever you went to school. It does not make you a leader. True leadership doesn't require a college education or even a high school education. True leadership requires self-education.

"The world is full of educated derelicts" (Calvin Coolidge, thirtieth president of the United States).[7]

I've known Allen for over twenty-five years. He is a great guy. I got to know him not long after I started working in church ministry. When he joined our staff, he had a bachelor's degree and two master's degrees in his field. Although he had only held one job very briefly in between his degrees, on paper he looked magnificent. He was a perfect fit for this job. He had all of the knowledge and background.

After about a month, I began to recognize that Allen had issues relating to people interpersonally. At times, he was abrupt and rude. He also (although he was in his thirties) seemed to view appointments, as well as completing his work on time, as optional. He was almost continuously late. When he wouldn't show up, he used the same excuses you would hear a college student use for not showing up for a class.

Now, once he was actually in his setting, he knew more than everybody about the subject matter. I don't mean that sarcastically; he really did know the material. He was one of the most knowledgeable, intelligent people I've ever met. But the way he conveyed that knowledge came across as arrogant and condescending. The people didn't connect with him.

Allen came to me six months into the job and informed me that he needed a raise. He had acquired massive school debt (well into six figures). Mind you, that school debt had been incurred for a degree in a field where the average pay was about 20 percent annually of what he owed.

Within a year, Allen approached me and informed me—you guessed it—that he was returning to school to pursue another master's degree. He knew if he went back to school, the debt would be deferred, and he could get more education.

Allen had all the education he needed to be qualified in his field of study. Actually, he had *more* training than he needed to be qualified; he just possessed none of the necessary skills to relate to people and to lead them.

Just because a person has a degree, doesn't mean they are a leader.

> "The world is full of educated derelicts."

My father was a graduate and undergraduate professor for more than thirty years. I understand the value of education. But I also know there are things you cannot learn in a school classroom. Many situations require practical application.

Here's the hard truth: Education can get you a job, but self-education can get you a *fortune*.

Jim Rohn said, "Work on yourself harder than your work on your job."[8] He also encouraged people to work full-time on their job and part-time on their fortune. The most significant investment you can ever make is not in real estate or the stock market or in a 401K. The greatest investment you can ever make is in yourself! So, the questions are:

- How much time do you spend working on *you*?

- Do you have a systematic plan in place to grow yourself?

- Do you have goals written out for your life for the next five years? The next week?

I would guess that you, like most people, have a dream for your life you'd like to see fulfilled. Here's a quick way to see if you're on that personal growth path or not:

1) Write out your life goal(s). As the author of *The 7 Habits of Highly Effective People*, Stephen Covey said, "Start with the end in mind." Ask yourself: At the end of your life, what would you like to have accomplished? At your funeral, what would you want those closest to you to say about you? What would you like to have written on your epitaph?

2) Look at that goal and begin to divide it out. What do you need to accomplish in the next ten years to move toward those goals? How about the next five years? How about the next twelve months?

3) Now I want you to do something a little radical: I want you to take the next week and (within reason!) write down everything you do. Write down when you get up, when you eat, when you work, when you watch TV, when you exercise, when you go to bed—*everything*. Take an entire week and be as meticulous as you can with this list. Use a

weekly planner if you have one. It'll help you track it, and it's easy to carry with you for a week.

4) At the end of that week (here comes the hard part!), take the goals for your life that you wrote out and the list of things you actually did last week and compare the two. How much of what you actually did in that previous week moved you toward your goals?

5) If you're on track for your goals, good for you! If you not, you now know where you need to make your adjustments.

6) Did you put aside some time in your schedule to grow yourself? Are you reading inspiring books? Are you listening to inspirational speakers who will help you grow mentally, physically, and spiritually? If not, add those in as priorities! Remember, as you grow, so does everything else.

> ## How much time do you spend working on *you*?

Your income will very often match your personal growth. I don't know why this is true, but it very often is. As you grow personally and become more, your opportunities for income and advancement will also grow with you. They just do.

How many times have we heard of a lottery winner who wins over $100 million? Most people would say, "If I had half of that money, I would be set for life!" Actually, that is not necessarily true. The majority of these lottery winners are broke and bankrupt within five years of winning that money.[9] Why? Personal growth! Their growth did not match their income. When that is the case, the money will always drop to the level of personal growth.

Now commit to yourself and your loved ones that you will give 100 percent every day to these goals. What you don't give today cannot be made up tomorrow. I heard a story about legendary UCLA basketball coach John Wooden. One of his players on the practice court was only giving about 80 percent. When Coach Wooden called him out on it, the player replied that he wasn't feeling well and would give Coach Wooden 120 percent tomorrow, when he felt better. Coach Wooden took him off the court and informed him, "The most you can ever give is 100 percent. There is no such thing as giving 120 percent. What you don't give today can never be made up tomorrow."

We have to give it our all every day!

Don't throw your education in someone else's face. Let your actions speak for themselves. Having knowledge is great but, as far as leadership goes, that knowledge is only as good as how you use it to benefit others. Whether you have a degree or not, spend time working on *you*. The time you spend working on yourself and your personal growth will yield incredible results in your life if applied consistently over time. Personal growth is your key to unlock the door to your dreams and your destiny! Remember, "People would rather learn from a non-professional DOER than a professional teacher." (Dean Graziosi.)[10]

Your income will very often match
your personal growth.

# CHAPTER 6

# MY TALENT MAKES ME WORTHY OF LEADERSHIP

## LEADERSHIP ILLUSION # 4

**T**he Effect: The person who has the most gifts, talents, and abilities should naturally be the leader.

**The Secret:** Talent does not entitle a person to anything. They may have gifts and abilities, but leadership is not a talent. It is an acquired skill.

Kevin Durant, the NBA star, knew, "Hard work beats talent when talent doesn't work hard."[11] Very early on, my oldest son, Drew, was labeled a "slow learner." Often the butt of his friends' jokes, he endured lots of insults. While some of his friends didn't even have to try to make As on their tests, Drew had to struggle for every grade he got. And sometimes, working as hard as he could, his best grade was a C. He also had a speech impediment that prevented him from saying certain consonants.

When he was asked to stand up in front of a group and read, it was particularly brutal. He read one word at a time very slowly in a monotone voice. This would often elicit laughter from the other kids. I remember the day he came home and told me, "Dad, I'm just dumb."

I asked him where he'd heard that. He replied, "My friends tell me all the time. I've just finally believed it."

I was shocked. I was mad at the cruelty of his friends. I found out that during the course of a play he had been in (at a church, no less), his friends had called him "dumb," as well as "untalented." They told him he couldn't sing, he couldn't act, and nobody could understand him when he talked because at age ten, he still "talked like a baby."

His self-esteem was destroyed. He told me, "Dad, they're just good. They've always been good. I'm not."

I sat him down and told him a story. It's one you've probably heard before, but it bears mentioning here: I asked him if he would rather have $2 million cash *or* a penny that doubles itself every day over the period of thirty days. He looked at me a little curiously and then wisely answered, "I'm not sure." (He knew I was up to something.) I told him that $2 million sounded great, *but* if you took a penny and began doubling it every day for thirty days then, after seventeen days (more than half!), it would only be worth $655.36. After twenty-two days, it would only be worth $20,971.52— compared to $2 million! *But* in the next eight days, that penny that would keep doubling and would end up being worth $5,368,709.12!

Then I told Drew that people are a lot like those two choices. Some people have gifts and abilities that make them seem like they're worth more, but the problem with those people is that they often don't work on their abilities. They simply coast on their talents and never develop beyond what they've been naturally given. Then there are the people who work hard all of their lives. They work on developing their strengths. Inevitably, they pass the talented people. In fact, they often leave the "talent-only" people in the dust. Talent alone cannot be relied upon.

Drew immediately understood. He began working on his speech. We took him to a speech therapist regularly. He also began studying but, after getting him tested, we realized he had a learning disability.

Whereas most people can look at a sentence and their brains can absorb the words, Drew had to read the words individually. His issue was called "binocularity," and it meant his eyes weren't working together. Where most people can go to a 3D movie and see in 3D with the special glasses, Drew could not because his eyes didn't work in conjunction with each other. We went through more therapy to correct that. For every inch of ground Drew gained, he had to work for it—extremely hard. But, fortunately, he did it!

But perhaps the most significant breakthrough for Drew came four years later in the form a despicable bully. The kid was three years older than Drew and a good foot taller. Drew would come home with bruises and scratch marks where the bully had picked on him and hit him. I decided the best route would be to take him to karate for lessons in self-defense. It was a huge turning point for him.

To say that he took to martial arts immediately would be a gross understatement. He latched onto the concepts and absorbed them. I was taking the classes with him, and his skill level exceeded mine from the get-go. Drew practiced karate and judo for multiple hours every day in order to improve. After taking lessons for about thirteen months, the bully was continuing his onslaught. One day, Drew came home with scratch marks around his neck where the bully had choked him.

I decided to have a word with the bully's parents. Their response was, "I know you haven't raised a boy yet, but this is very normal. Boys will be boys!" I couldn't believe it. So I pulled Drew aside and told him, "The next time that guy does something to you physically, you have my permission to get him off of you. Just don't break any bones."

In another few days, the inevitable happened: The bully attacked Drew from behind, putting him in a chokehold. Drew reversed the hold, rolled the boy over his shoulder and planted him on the ground.

The bully started screaming as Drew then put him into an armbar and said, "Are you going to ever touch me or my friends again?!" The bully screamed "*No*! Just let me go!" which Drew did immediately.

Now, I am not advocating violence to solve problems, but I do believe there are times when you have to stand up to the bullies in your life. And I'd be lying if I said I didn't feel a certain amount of satisfaction in what he did. The bully never bothered Drew or his friends again. Funny thing: The boy's parents approached me a couple of days after the incident and said, "This is getting a little out of hand!" I calmly replied, "Well, you know ... boys will be boys!" I know that was bad. Sorry ...

Drew went on to compete in the North American Grappling Association National Tournament in Atlanta. He won the fourteen-to-fifteen-year-old national championship, defeating opponents from all over the world.

I remember him holding his sword (that was the trophy they gave him) in the air and looking at me and smiling broadly. After going through those events, Drew cared less and less what some of his "friends" thought. He distanced himself from those who attempted to make fun of him just to make themselves look good. He grew to realize that insecure people often put others down in a vain attempt to make themselves look better. He had no bad feelings toward them, but he also understood the importance of surrounding himself with true friends who build each other up.

Drew graduated high school with a GPA of 3.6. He went on to a local university and got a degree in accounting with a 3.9 GPA. Seven months before he graduated from college, he received a lucrative offer to work in one of the largest accounting firms in the world.

I tell you the story of my son to make this point: Hard work beats talent every time. Hard work offers rewards that talent never will. I'm proud of my son, who has lived this truth out in his own life.

Dino Kartsonakis is arguably one of the best piano players of our time. He has been a featured artist all over the world, including Las Vegas, and had his own show in Branson, Missouri. He has been consistently at the top of that genre for over fifty years. I spoke with him recently and he told me that, at the age of seventy-six, he still practices several hours a day! What a great example to all of us! Even someone who is considered a virtuoso of his instrument still works on his craft for several hours a day to stay sharp and continually improve.

> Hard work beats talent every time. Hard work offers rewards that talent never will.

Every one of us has some sort of gifting, talent, or ability. Some have more than others; some have less. The key isn't what we're given. The key is what we do with what we're given. Here are a few recommendations:

1) Whatever talents and abilities you have, determine right now to work on them and develop them more. Don't rest on your laurels. Don't rest on your natural gifts. Study harder. Work harder. The more you work on your strengths, the better chance you have of standing out and the more people you will be able to help.

2) Whatever weaknesses you have, realize you can improve on them, but you'll probably never be great at them. I've found it's infinitely better to delegate or hire my weaknesses than it is to spend all of my time trying to improve them.

**3)** Realize that the unseen work you do is far more important than what others see. It's a sad truth but, the majority of the time, the people we see on a stage or screen bear little resemblance to who they actually are in private. If we are going to succeed, it's going to take hard work that nobody sees. Everyone loves to compliment someone who lost weight. For some people, it might seem like an overnight transformation. But the person who lost the weight knows of the times they spent fixing meals that nourished their bodies and supported their weight loss. They also know of the countless hours they spent exercising just to lose half a pound. The hard work in secret will yield huge benefits in public. "The fight is won or lost far away from witnesses—behind the lines, in the gym, and out there on the road, long before I dance under those lights" (Muhammad Ali).[12]

**4)** Ask yourself what your gifts or talents are, then write down ways they could be used to serve others. The greatest benefits of your talents are not in how they can help *you*; the benefits are always in how your gifts or talents can serve others and add value to them!

> The key isn't what we're given.
> The key is what we do with what we're given.

Determine today that you will not rest on any gifts or talents you've been given. Decide that you will work hard on developing those talents even further. As the Bible says in Luke 12:48, "For everyone to whom much is given, from him much will be required; and to whom much has been committed, of him, they will ask the more."

If you've been given a lot of gifts and talents then more is required of you. If you've been given one talent, the mandate is still the same: work hard on it and develop it.

"Nothing is more common than talented unsuccessful men." (Calvin Coolidge, thirtieth president of the United States.)[13] Determine today not to be one of the common people who never develop or work hard on their talents. Decide right now that you will be one of the ones who out-works everyone else and moves from success to significance and leaves a lasting impact upon the lives of others.

"Nothing is more common than talented unsuccessful men."

# CHAPTER 7

# I Don't Need Anyone to Help Me

---
LEADERSHIP ILLUSION # 5
---

**T**he Effect: You can get to your goals and achieve success by yourself. You don't need anybody else!

**The Secret:** Nobody has achieved any significant measure of success by themselves. It simply doesn't happen.

Jonathan (not his real name) was in a direct sales company. That entire business (which I do love, by the way) is built on the premise of building a "downline" of people whose income and activities will eventually lead to residual income for you. Do it long enough and successfully enough and it can provide a lucrative, residual passive income for the rest of your life. Many successful entrepreneurs (like Jim Rohn, for instance) have started their road to financial freedom through a direct sales company.

Jonathan had spent his life working for money. He saw the value of direct sales and how he could make an incredible income with this particular company, so he went to work. The person who signed him up had achieved the top level in the company in eighteen months and challenged Jonathan to do it faster than he had.

Jonathan had a background in sports and was widely known for being aggressive. He brought that same aggressiveness to his new business, and he took off like a rocket. The next several months were a whirlwind of activity. He was signing people up like a maniac!

And nearly every person he signed up, he challenged them to build the business rapidly, just like he was.

Things were moving along nicely, and he was right on track to beat his sponsor's record. He was making a lot of money and was quickly becoming the "poster boy" for the entire company.

But there were a few issues ...

First of all, Jonathan had a tendency to sign people up by using high-pressure tactics on them and then, once they were signed up, he tended not to speak to them—that is, unless he deemed they needed help. Coincidentally, the ones who often "needed his help" seemed to always be the ones who would pay him the most money. Some people felt used, as if he'd only signed them up as a "number" and didn't care about them personally.

Jonathan also had a problem relating to people who thought differently than he did. If somebody didn't take to his forceful challenges at the beginning, they ended up being labeled as "lazy" or even "losers" who had no drive to succeed. He pressed on. Nothing was going to stop him from reaching his goal. He would often say, "I don't need them anyway! I'm going to get this done with or without them!"

He pressed on, full force, guns blazing. And yes—he made it. He beat the record and went to the very top of the company. He made a ton of money. By all outside appearances, it seemed like a tremendous success story.

But there was a significant problem. He had reached his goal and (in his mind) built a large direct sales business with lots of people in his downline. The residual income side of this business is built on the presupposition that the people in the downline will continue working and signing people up. But the people Jonathan had used to achieve his goal felt exactly that way—used.

Not only were they not aggressively pursuing the business as he had, but they were also dropping out altogether, some of them filled with considerable resentment. Jonathan ignored them or criticized them publicly for having bad attitudes and for not having a "winner" mentality. Some team members stuck by him, sharing his dream of building a business for their families. However, Jonathan became lax in helping them as he had promised he would.

He reasoned, "I spent almost two years building this, now I'm going to enjoy the fruits of my labor!" He missed promised phone calls and scheduled meetings. Because he had reached the top so quickly, he was featured in several publications, and he became even more arrogant. He saw many in his downline as a distraction to "his" success.

It doesn't take a rocket scientist to guess that most of his downline quit to pursue other business ventures. Jonathan saw the handwriting on the wall as his checks deteriorated along with his downline. He had broken a cardinal rule of direct sales: You have to build leadership in your downline, and you need people to make that happen. It's a relationship business.

Jonathan ended up leaving that direct sales company for another "up-and-coming" company he had previously railed against. He recruited heavily in his downline, but he had little luck getting people to follow him to another company because they had seen his selfish ambition in the previous one. That venture went south quickly, and he jumped into a couple of others. He received a lot of income at the beginning, but he failed to do the most important thing: build relationships and residual income. All of the income from the businesses he attempted dried up. The last I heard, Jonathan had a job in the retail industry and had sworn off direct sales as a "scam."

> He had broken a cardinal rule of direct sales: You have to build leadership in your downline.

Any significant business is built not only with commitment and tenacity, but with relationships with the right business partners and the right team. Nobody has ever achieved any considerable measure of success without an excellent team around them.

If you're going to achieve your goals, it's going to require a great team. Every president who achieved success had a great cabinet. Every successful corporation president had a great team. You and I are no different.

In thinking about what your goals are, ask yourself a few questions:

1)  What are my strengths and what are my weaknesses?

2)  Who do I know that is strong where I am weak?

3)  How can I add value to the people on my own team? What do they need?

4)  Who do I know that can add value to all of us and move us closer to the goal?

5)  Why am I not meeting with these people regularly?

Take some time and answer all of the above questions honestly. Write the answers down in the space provided or type them out (if that's easier for you).

> Nobody has ever achieved any considerable measure of success without an excellent team around them.

No matter who you are or what you're doing, if you're going to achieve measurable, lasting success in any industry or organization, you need a team around you that will help you succeed.

Remember, "One is too small a number to achieve greatness." (Dr. John C. Maxwell.)[14]

"One is too small a number to achieve greatness."

# CHAPTER 8

# IF IT WEREN'T FOR HIM, I WOULD'VE SUCCEEDED

## LEADERSHIP ILLUSION # 6

**T**he Effect: "People are keeping me from being successful. If they would just do what they were supposed to do or what they said they'd do, then I'd succeed." This effect also applies to those who don't complete their work or are consistently late, and they always have a reason why it isn't their fault.

**The Secret:** The "blame game" never works. We ultimately succeed when we take full responsibility for ourselves and our successes and failures. Our success is not up to anybody but us. The hard truth about the second part is that nobody truly cares *why* we were late or *why* we didn't get the job done. When it comes down to it, they're all excuses, and nobody likes, respects, or follows excuses. They follow leadership. Excuses spend our leadership influence like water flowing through a massive hole in a dam. It can take years to replenish what was spent by even just one excuse.

I heard a story about a man whose neighbor always wanted to borrow items from him but either wouldn't return them or, when he did, returned them damaged. One day, the neighbor asked the man if he could borrow his lawnmower. The man replied, "No. You can't borrow my lawnmower. I'm cooking spaghetti." The confused neighbor replied, "What does cooking spaghetti have to do with borrowing your lawnmower?" The man replied, "Nothing. I just don't want to let you borrow it, and I figured one excuse is as good as the next."

A person who needs an excuse will always find one.

I was sitting in a large room with about 2,500 people. It was our biannual meeting of the John Maxwell Team, and Dr. John Maxwell was on stage introducing this woman. He simply said, "I want to bring her up here and let you hear her story."

If you were to see Maria, you wouldn't think her to be the amazing woman she is. She's barely five feet tall and wiry. Nothing about her speech or look singles her out as someone incredible, but she is one of the most phenomenal, determined women I've ever met.

Maria was raised in Portugal but did not receive the same educational opportunities as other people. At a young age, she left home and trained to become a flight attendant, eventually working a very lucrative position for Emirates airlines. Her life was spent traveling from exotic country to exotic country, staying at posh hotels and enjoying a very nice life. That is, until twenty-four hours in Bangladesh changed her life forever.

Maria had taken a flight from Dubai to Dhaka. She spent twenty-four hours in that city and witnessed poverty on a scale she had never seen before. It moved her so profoundly that she decided she had to do something about it. She sold her clothes, jewelry, and all other items that had any value. She emptied her savings accounts and determined she was going to change the lives of 600 children in Dhaka.

At first, she was able to provide the proper vaccinations and other basic needs. With her connections in Dubai, she knew some people who had money, but this was 2008, and the Great Recession caused all of her funding sources to dry up. Many would have used that as an excuse to quit. She could have returned to her flight attendant position and made money for herself, but she had a dream of helping these children get the proper vaccinations, clothing, and education all the way through high school. She calculated the cost to provide these needs for all 600 kids at $1.3 million.

Unaware of what to do, Maria Googled, "How do you make a million dollars?"

The first thing that caught her eye was climbing Mount Everest. If she successfully made it the summit, she could get $1 million. And so … she did it. She became the first Portuguese woman to make it to the top of Mount Everest. But the funding failed to come through.

So again, she Googled, "How do you make a million dollars?"

The next thing that caught her eye was a corporation that would sponsor her for $750,000 if she successfully made it to the North Pole. And so … she did it. But the recession hit that corporation, and she didn't get her money then either.

Many people would have given up at this point, but not Maria. She again searched on the internet for ways to make money and discovered she could be paid a lot of money for swimming across the English Channel. There was just one problem: Maria couldn't swim.

She approached a swim coach and asked if he could train her to swim across the English Channel. He told her that he had never done anything like that before. It was a twenty-one-mile swim. He told her that he could teach her how to swim but to train her to swim the English Channel would take at least two years. Maria told him those children wouldn't wait that long and gave him six months.

In six months, yes—she swam across the English Channel. But the current was strong that day and moved her to a different point than where she was supposed to land, and so she didn't receive the money.

So again (you guessed it!), Google told her if she did the Ironman marathon on every continent within a certain amount of time, she would receive a large sum of money. So she trained and did it.

Today, Maria Cristina holds *eight* records in *The Guinness Book of World Records*. But she didn't want any of that. She simply wanted to help 600 children living an impoverished existence get the help they needed. Through her efforts and her unwillingness to accept any excuses or setbacks, she was able to raise $1 million. This left her $300,000 short.

As I listened to this incredibly moving story, I watched people in the room begin to stand up and spontaneously walk to the stage and throw money on the platform. Nobody asked them to do a thing. It just happened. I participated in the giving. In just ten minutes, there were two hefty-sized garbage bags full of cash. At the end of the day, over $149,000 had been raised for the Maria Cristina Foundation.[15] I, along with many others, watched through tears as John Maxwell pledged to help her raise the other $151,000.

Those 600 children in Dhaka, Bangladesh, are now receiving the education and care they need. Maria lives there and helps those children herself. All of the money given to her foundation goes to help the children. If you're interested in donating, you can find out more at www.mariacristinafoundation.org.

Maria could have let a myriad of excuses stop her, but she refused to accept any of them. She pressed forward with determination and incredible willpower for one reason: those children. She didn't care about conquering Mount Everest or swimming the English Channel. Those were simply a means to an end.

A dream or a goal that has a powerful "why" will always find a way. It will never let something as flimsy as an excuse stand in its way.

An hour or so after our session, I ran into Maria in the hallway. I stopped and had my photo taken with her. I told her how she had inspired me, and I also told her of a few dreams of my own that I wanted to accomplish.

With her tiny frame facing me, she raised her index finger to my face and said only two words in her Portuguese accent: "No excuses."

Excuses are easy to find. They're easy for our minds to accept too. In fact, our thoughts gravitate toward them. It's easy to find a reason why something didn't happen the way we thought it should or even blame someone else as the reason our lives didn't turn out the way we wanted them to. The actual reason we look for excuses is simply that they alleviate the pain of accepting responsibility for our current circumstances and/or condition. The easiest thing to do in the morning is to roll over and say, "I'm tired. I'll exercise later today." (Which often turns into tomorrow, and the next day, and the next day …) It's easy to say, "I'll start eating right tomorrow. After all, I just blew my diet with that french fry. I might as well just have an entire meal." It's easy to say, "I know I should apologize to them, but they won't receive it anyway. I'll waste my time, and I'll look like an idiot too. Besides, they should be apologizing to me!" It's easy to say, "I know I'm in debt, so another hundred dollars won't hurt me on that credit card." It's easy to give ourselves permission to do nearly anything.

> A dream or a goal that has a powerful "why" will always find a way.

Again, excuses are a dime a dozen.

But the truth is, the blame for our circumstances almost always lies at our own feet. And the responsibility for getting to where we want or need to be *always* lies at our feet. Regardless of our circumstances, we have to take ownership of our own lives to get to where we need to be.

Here are some steps to take today:

1) Decide today to take responsibility for your own destiny. Regardless of what has been done to you, regardless of what has happened to you, regardless of what others have said or done, *you* take responsibility. The moment you do this is a huge moment of empowerment for you. You are no longer a slave to the "blame game," and your dreams and destiny are no longer chained to someone else's actions or opinions. The moment we blame others for our station in life is the moment we take the keys to our life and willingly hand them over to other people (most likely, ones who don't care for us, and we probably don't care for them) to drive us around to whatever destination they choose for us. Don't give away your keys!

2) Realize that the only person you can change is you. In my years of doing marriage counseling, I cannot count the number of couples where one spouse would say, "I just know they'll change after I marry them," or "I know I can change them!" Guess what happened? Yep—no change. The hard truth is that you cannot change anybody except *you*. What areas of your life do you need to change?

3) Make a list of "excuse" and "blame" areas in your life. Get a separate piece of paper and answer the following questions: In what areas do you blame others for a lack of results in your life, and in what areas have you used excuses to justify your current circumstances? This is a painful exercise to do, but it's necessary for your freedom! Be honest and open. Nobody is seeing this list except you.

4) Now for the important part: Go through each and every excuse you've just written and then write the following three words over every one of them: "I AM RESPONSIBLE!" Doing this easy but powerful exercise

can free you from the chains of excuses and move you to where you've wanted to be.

5) Realize that any "excuse" we use is our own lack of willpower trying to keep us from achieving our personal goals. You have to be stronger than that lack of willpower. Lack of willpower will throw every excuse in your corner and fight you every day. The more you defeat it on a daily basis, the weaker it becomes. The more you allow it to win, the stronger it becomes. Knock it down—*today*!

> ## Excuses are a dime a dozen.

This reminds me of a story I heard about two dogs fighting. One was a Doberman, and the other was a German Shepherd. Which one won? The one that was fed the most. What you feed will win. Whatever you water in your life will grow.

If you just read those questions above and are about to go on without answering them, please don't. Stop and really write them down. None of us need to finish a book just for the sake of finishing it. We need true transformation! Don't let an excuse keep you away from the person you're supposed to be any longer.

The easiest thing to do is access an excuse just to go ahead and finish this chapter quickly. Don't do it! Break that habit starting now. If you'll write down the answers to those questions and then write "I AM RESPONSIBLE" over them, you'll be well on your way to breaking the power of excuses in your life and empowering yourself for success in leadership and in life.

While hiking in the Tennessee mountains, I saw a river flowing that dropped off a small cliff onto a boulder. I saw a large hole in the rock about the size of a soccer ball that the water had cut into it.

A large hole through an actual boulder! That hole hadn't been cut by the power of the water; it had been cut by the *persistence* of the water. It had been cut because the water kept hitting the same spot over and over for decades.

The same is true for us. If we don't accept excuses but press forward and keep going, there is no excuse that we cannot conquer.

The bottom line is, we can make progress or we can make excuses, but we cannot do both. The choice is ours. The ball is in our court. The only question is, will we accept responsibility and move forward into our destinies?

Determine today to take responsibility for your own actions. Beat the tar out of your lack of willpower. Beat that punk into submission. Don't accept excuses and don't blame others for where you are. You are worth it! Your dream is worth it! You can do it!

Adopt the motto for your own life given to me by Maria Cristina: "No excuses!"

> We can make progress or we can make excuses, but we cannot do both.

# CHAPTER 9

# JUST IGNORE IT. IT'LL GET BETTER.

**T**he **Effect**: If you ignore things, they usually get better. Just like a fine wine, almost everything improves over time, including people.

**The Secret**: Everything decays with age. Nothing ever improves on its own.

I have a friend who bought a boat a few years ago. He was so excited! He bought it in April, right before peak boating season here in Tennessee. That summer, he was out on his boat nearly every weekend and many weekdays. He really enjoyed that summer. The next summer, he was pretty busy. He took the boat out five times that summer. The next *two* summers, the boat stayed in the dock, and he didn't go out on it at all. He was traveling. He was working. He was just "too busy."

The following summer, some of his family wanted to use the boat. But it was covered in bugs and had some mold on the upholstery. The engine also wouldn't start. He brought a guy out to look at the boat. Letting it sit in the water for two years hadn't helped it at all. He was told he should've gone out and started the engine some. The bottom line was it needed work—a *lot* of work. So … he sold it.

He told me that the old adage was true: "The second greatest day of your life is when you buy your boat. The greatest day of your life is when you sell it." He took a loss on it and didn't care. He was just happy that it was done and he was rid of it.

Imagine buying a brand-new car and then leaving it sitting in your front yard for thirty years. You never wash it. Never drive it. Never even start it. Can you imagine what kind of condition that car would be in thirty years later? It would be covered in rust and mold, and the engine would likely be destroyed. Actually, if you drive around some rural regions in Tennessee, you can actually see lots of old cars sitting up on blocks in people's front yards!

Take a beautiful polished silver platter and leave it outside for ten years. It will look tarnished and worn and will have lost its luster and likely be permanently damaged. Leave a piece of shiny metal outside for years and rust will completely cover it and, eventually, destroy it.

I have also watched people do this with their lives. I've seen people smoke themselves or eat themselves into an early grave. I've watched people ignore their financial situation, only to lose their house and end up bankrupt. I've watched people neglect important relationships and end up losing them. I could go on and on with examples, and so could you.

The point is clear: Nothing improves through ignoring it. *Nothing*. Everything decays with age and neglect. And yet, even facing this obvious truth, we do the same thing to ourselves! We neglect our own growth. We neglect our health. We neglect our essential relationships. We neglect our work and our business. We neglect our money.

Sometimes, a person's temperament keeps them from confronting these all-critical issues. Other times, it is sheer laziness or apathy. Whatever the reason, we can know for sure that nothing in our lives will improve by neglecting it. We must be intentional about our own personal growth. If we aren't intentional about it, we can be sure nobody else will do it for us.

Personal growth will determine how far we go in life. As a matter of fact, your own personal growth will almost always be reflected in the amount of money you make. I had a multimillionaire tell me one time (while I was on his huge houseboat), "The more I work on my personal growth, the more money I make. When I don't work on my personal growth, my income always goes down to match it." A person's monetary worth will always match their personal growth habits. We touched on this in Chapter 6.

Please note: I said *monetary* worth. I do not believe that a person's *personal* worth is wrapped up in the amount of money they have. I believe personal worth is an entirely different issue. But in this case, I'm speaking solely of monetary worth and its relationship to personal growth.

This book is about leadership. I believe that an individual who does not invest in themselves and their personal growth is not qualified to be a leader of anyone.

Dr. John C. Maxwell said, "Leaders know the way, show the way, and go the way."[16] If you haven't been going the way of personal growth, how you can expect those people you are supposed to be influencing to grow? You cannot lead where you haven't been.

There is also a Maxwell Law from his book, *The 21 Irrefutable Laws of Leadership*, in play here. Law #1 is the Law of the Lid, which states, "Leadership ability is the lid that determines a person's level of effectiveness." In other words, if a person's leadership ability is a six, then the highest their organization will ever rise to is a five. If the leader is an eight, then the organization can only rise to a seven. If the leader is a three, then the organizational leadership can only rise to a two.

Do you see why it is critical to work on yourself and your personal growth? Everyone you influence and lead is counting on you to grow. And, as you grow, so goes the organization and people you lead.

> ## Nothing improves through ignoring it. *Nothing.*

"You cannot hope to build a better world without improving the individuals. To that end, each of us must work for our own improvement and, at the same time, share a general responsibility for all humanity, our particular duty being to aid those to whom we think we can be most useful." (Madame Marie Curie.) [17]

In order for you to grow, you need an intentional plan. It won't happen by accident. Here are four steps to grow in your awareness and intentionality in your personal growth. And remember, "Work on yourself harder than you work on your job." (Jim Rohn.) [18]

1) **Be proactive!** Again, nobody is going to do this for you—not your family, not your spouse, not your trainer, and definitely not your boss at work. In fact, do you know what your work has planned for you in your personal growth? If it's like most places, not much. So, determine now that you will have a personal growth plan. Go get a pen and paper, and let's write down a few things.

2) **Write down some areas you've neglected in your life.** What are the areas that need attention? Your health? Your family? Your relationships? Your spiritual life? Your work? Your dreams? Your finances? Your life's purpose and goals? Now is the time for brutal honesty with yourself. Nobody is going to see this list but you. We all have to start somewhere, and that "somewhere" means being brutally honest. For

some, that might mean getting on the scale for the first time in several years. For others, it might mean doing a financial report of income vs. expenses and assets vs. liabilities. It might mean having a difficult conversation with a loved one. Always remember for this stage that it is much better and healthier for us to acknowledge the truth of where we are, rather than to ignore it and continue to live a lie. This is really a huge key to moving to where you've always wanted to go. Ignoring it never fixes it.

3) **Ask yourself what it would take to improve by 1 percent in that area (or areas) every week.** Notice that I didn't say 5 percent or 10 percent. I said only 1 percent. Write it down. In other words, if being healthier was your goal and you wanted to improve by just 1 percent, you could commit to eating smaller portions or even going for a walk twice a week. We're not talking a lot. If your goal was to improve your finances, instead of getting that cup of coffee at that large chain coffee shop that costs you from seven to ten dollars a day, fix your own coffee and take that money and put it toward a credit card bill. There are all sorts of little adjustments that can be made. Again, we're talking 1 percent! Do you want to grow in the area of spirituality? Read a book in that area. Just do a chapter a day or even just one section of a chapter. Read a motivational book at night or listen to a motivational podcast or CD on the way to work every day. There are so many ways to implement these small changes! I personally read the Bible and meditate on the meaning of the verses. We'll talk more about the power of these little decisions in the next chapter but, for now, just realize that small decisions today have huge implications in the future. Just think: If you improve by 1 percent every week then, in one year, you will have developed that area by 50 percent! (I'm giving you two weeks off for vacation!) That's *huge* progress!

4) **Add the 1 percent improvements to your daily "to-do" list.** Here is where we get more practical. If these decisions are not added to what you're doing every day then we haven't gotten anywhere. We haven't made any real changes. Some people have a personality that leads them to try to do too much too soon. You don't have to do that. Take small steps. Small adjustments today will lead to great rewards tomorrow. Is it easy? Well, kind of. Yes, it's easy to do. The problem is, it's also easy *not* to do. Most people choose the latter because it's more comfortable and doesn't require any change on our part. Anything worthwhile we do in our lives requires us to make sacrifices and work hard. We just have to make the choice actually to do it.

> "You cannot hope to build a better world without improving the individuals."

Master magician Harry Houdini was once asked, "Is there something foundational for the magician that is similar to scales for the musician?"[19] (In other words, is there something that sets the stage for everything else a magician does?) Houdini chose this effect. It is over 3,000 years old. It originated in ancient Egypt. In modern times, it evolved into a street swindle. The effect is known as the "Cups and Balls," and is still performed today by many magicians.

The basic setup is two or three cups that have small balls placed inside them. The balls disappear and reappear under the cups. Typically, the climactic end of the effect is that a large object appears magically under the cups. Houdini said, "I consider no man to be a magician who cannot perform this effect proficiently."[20]

Years ago, I determined I was going to learn it. I found a magician who was known as the resident expert in this effect. His name is Michael Ammar, and he is considered one of the greatest teachers of magic in the world. He produced some videos on the "Cups and Balls" and wrote several books about it. Not only did I study all of those, but I also contacted him personally and asked him to teach and mentor me in this effect. To my shock, he agreed.

The first time I showed it to Michael (after six months of work, mind you!), I had learned several things completely wrong and had to unlearn and relearn several parts. This is a particularly difficult thing for me to do. It took me two years to learn the effect proficiently enough that I could actually show someone. It has now become a staple in every illusion show I do, and it often receives a standing ovation. The entire effect lasts less than three minutes, and most people have no clue about the years of practice, the hundreds of separate moves, and the years and years of refining that have gone into that one effect.

But that's the value of hard work and personal growth: Most people will never know how hard a person has worked to achieve success. To them, it seems effortless. They are the people who are incredible speakers, athletes, musicians, actors, teachers, dancers, magicians, and singers of whom the world says, "They make that look so easy!"

We've all heard of people called "overnight successes." I would say there is no such thing. They might have achieved overnight *fame*, but there is really no such thing as an overnight success.

They are simply bamboo trees. A bamboo tree is planted, and for the first year is watered and cultivated but never appears above the ground. The second year comes and goes. Nothing—not a sprout. The third year, same thing. Fourth year, still nothing. But in the fifth year, something magical happens: That tree shoots through the ground and grows *eighty feet* in *six weeks*.

But now the question: Did it grow eighty feet in six weeks, or did it grow eighty feet in five years? Some people might suppose it took only six weeks to grow that tree, but they would be wrong. The foundational growth over five years was essential.

The same is true of you. You may have already been working on your personal growth. There may be no visible outward signs to people who are looking at you, your life, your finances, or other areas. But *you* know you're changing. *You* know you're making progress and growing. Others may make fun of you. They may say it will never happen. They may say, "Look at all the money and time you've wasted on personal growth, and you haven't changed at all!" They see no signs of the bamboo tree that is growing beneath the surface. Others may laugh at you. They won't be laughing when that bamboo shoots out of the ground! And then they'll all be astounded and call you "lucky" or even an "overnight success."

But we'll both know better, won't we?

> They might have achieved overnight *fame*, but there is really no such thing as an overnight success.

# CHAPTER 10

# I'LL DO THAT TOMORROW

---

### LEADERSHIP ILLUSION # 8

---

**T**he Effect: "I'll get to that tomorrow."

**The Secret**: We can't be defeated by our pasts or obsessed with our futures. Our focus must be on the only day we can affect: today! The truth is, the "tomorrow" we're waiting for never gets here. More people are derailed in their leadership and in their success journey by this one thing: procrastination.

We've all heard about this issue, and you're in one of two categories. You're either that last-minute person who is always late and gets everything in just under the wire, *or* you're the person who is incredibly irritated by the individuals mentioned above.

But don't fret, procrastinators. You're definitely not alone. In fact, you're in some very famous company:

- **Herman Melville.** The American author reportedly had his wife chain him to his desk while he was struggling to finish his epic novel *Moby-Dick*. This method worked. The book, first published in 1851, is often listed among the greatest works of fiction ever written.[21]

- **Victor Hugo.** Okay, I'll just go ahead and admit this is extreme and unusual. But it worked. The great French poet and novelist, whose masterpieces include the epic historical novels *Les Misérables* and *The Hunchback of Notre-Dame*, had a unique method to stave off procrastination: He had his servant strip him naked in his study and not return with his clothes until the appointed hour. It prevented him from leaving his room. I guess extreme procrastination calls for extreme measures?[22]

- **Wolfgang Amadeus Mozart.** Arguably the greatest composer of all time, Mozart wrote the overture for *Don Giovanni* in a single night. Unfortunately, it was the night before the opera's debut! Granted, he was Mozart and was talented enough to pull it off. The thirty-one-year-old virtuoso would compose entire symphonies in his mind—often while playing billiards—and, at times, he didn't put pen to paper until he'd completed the entire piece in his head first. At *Don Giovanni*'s premiere, the ink on the overture's sheet music was still wet from its last-minute copying, and there was no time for rehearsal. "Some notes fell under the stands," Mozart said later, "but it went well."[23]

- **General George McClellan.** The North might have won the US Civil War a lot faster if not for the procrastination of General McClellan, who was renowned for his meticulous preparation of the Union army. "If he can't fight himself, he excels in making others ready to fight," Lincoln said of him. Except that the endless preparation was a form of procrastination: When the chips were down, McClellan couldn't bring himself to go into battle. This type of over-preparation and perfectionism often leads to "analysis paralysis." (More on that later...)

- **President Bill Clinton.** The then-vice president Al Gore described him as "punctually challenged" and, even though he was given months to complete important speeches, they were often done in the wee hours of the morning the night before.[24]

- **Emperor Marcus Aurelius.** Known as one of the greatest emperors of the Roman Empire, he said, "Think of all the years passed by in which you said to yourself 'I'll do it tomorrow,' and how the gods have again and again granted you periods of grace of which you have not availed yourself. It is time to realize that you are a member of the universe, that you are born of nature itself, and to know that a limit has been set to your time."[25]

- **The Dalai Lama.** "You must not procrastinate. Rather you should make preparations so that even if you die tonight, you would have no regrets."[26]

So, as you can see, procrastinators abound, as well as the people who are irritated by them. Many have struggled with putting things off. To be honest, I am writing this chapter a week later than I was supposed to. Procrastination is such an easy thing to do.

I'm not sure who said it, but it's very true: "Procrastination has taught me how to do eight hours of work in thirty minutes, as well as thirty minutes of work in eight hours."

Here is the truth: *Today matters*. What you did yesterday cannot be undone. What you're going to do tomorrow doesn't matter. It's what you do *today* that matters. Today is all you have control of. *Today* is all you can affect. And what you do *today* is what will make tomorrow what it is supposed to be.

Despite what you've put off for days, weeks, months, or years, *today* you can change all of that. Yesterday's failures don't matter. Neither do yesterday's victories, for that matter. Let's quickly define "tomorrow" in this context: "Tomorrow is the mystical land where almost all of human productivity, motivation, success, and achievement is stored, but extremely rarely harvested."

All we have is what we do today. The key to making tomorrow what it should be is to learn from what we did or didn't do yesterday and do today what will make our tomorrow what we want. But to do that, we must overcome procrastination. As Babe Ruth said, "Yesterday's home run won't win today's game."[27]

> What you did yesterday cannot be undone. What you're going to do tomorrow doesn't matter. It's what you do *today* that matters.

How do you overcome procrastination? Here are some brief and practical steps that have helped me in this area of my life:

1) **Make a list of things you've been putting off.** Really go for it. List those projects around the house, that big objective at work. What about that relationship you've been wanting to mend? The finances you know you need to get in order? Make a *full* list.

2) **List *one* step you can take in *one* area that will make a positive change in your life or move you closer to *one* of your goals.** Just one step, no more. Remember the last chapter: baby steps (yes, just like the movie *Groundhog Day*).

3) **Whatever that *one* thing is you just wrote down, *do it today*!** Not tomorrow—*today*. If you're reading this late at night or you're in a place where you can't physically complete that one thing, pick one you *can* do today and then do it.

4) **Learn that everything we do today will compound.** Albert Einstein said, "Compound interest is the eighth wonder of the world. He who understands it earns it … He who doesn't pays it."[28] Our lives are much like compound interest. Whether we know it or not, every action we take or do not take compounds in our lives. Show me a person who has no money and I'll show you someone who has made a series of

bad financial decisions for years that led to those circumstances. Show me a person who is very overweight and I'll show you a person who consistently ate things they should not have eaten and/or someone who doesn't exercise consistently. Show me a person who cannot hold a job and I'll show you a person who hasn't been working on their own personal growth for years. And before the emails start flying, I realize that life happens to everyone. Adverse circumstances happen, and I realize that the previous sentences contain some generalizations that do not apply to everyone. However, although it isn't true of every single person, it is true of most. Every decision we make compounds. The problem with compounding is that the pain and reward of that effect aren't instantly felt. In other words, when you eat that large piece of chocolate cake, you don't immediately gain twenty pounds. What a difference that would make in our eating habits! When you put that large purchase on a credit card that you will "eventually" pay off, your credit score doesn't immediately drop, and you don't see the bill for thirty days. But every little decision we make compounds and eventually turns us into who we will become, good or bad. Chris Widener said, "The actions you choose each and every day will add up, over the long term, to your final destination."[29] Will Durant, in his book about Aristotle, summed up the philosopher by saying, "Excellence then is not an act. Excellence is a habit."[30] Our lives are in our hands, and it's up to us to create habits of excellence. We do that by doing something today!

5) **Once you've accomplished the task, write down steps you can take in other areas.** Put them on your daily "to-do" list. Realize that, just as you accomplished the previous task, you can also achieve this one. Every task is doable by simply breaking it down into small steps and actually taking the steps every day!

> "Yesterday's home run won't win today's game."

"Action is a great restorer and builder of confidence. Inaction is not only the result of, but the case of, fear." (Dr. Norman Vincent Peale.)[31] Yes, that's really all there is to it. The cure for procrastination is action. It doesn't have to be massive action at first; that can lead to becoming overwhelmed and doing nothing. Just small steps in the right direction are the way to go.

One additional note: If you're a perfectionist, then waiting until everything is "perfect" is the quickest road to never getting it done at all. Most of the time, perfectionism is a veiled form of procrastination. They are at the very least first cousins and, more than likely, brothers. In other words, if you wait until the time is perfect for getting married, buying a house, having a baby, taking that vacation, going to your child's game or event, or having that tough conversation to reconcile a relationship, then you probably never will.

I'm not suggesting being foolish and running headlong into something completely unprepared, but there is such a thing as overpreparing and underdelivering. There is no such thing as the "perfect" time. That, my friend, is another illusion. It doesn't exist.

Incidentally, for all those procrastinators who flipped ahead in the book to see how long this chapter would take to read, it's one of the shortest chapters in the book on purpose. Yep. You're welcome.

Now, seriously: Go do that one thing. Do it now! Put this book down and get that one thing done. You'll be on the road to putting away procrastination for good, and you'll become a strong person of action! With a little bit of discipline added to your life combined with consistency, you will get there.

"In reading the lives of great men, I found that the first victory they won was over themselves… self-discipline with all of them came first." (Harry S. Truman)[32]

Remember, "We will all experience one of two great pains in life. The pain of discipline or the pain of regret. The pain of discipline weighs ounces. The pain of regret weighs tons." (Jim Rohn.)[33] Which pain are you going to choose today?

Also remember, "Inaction breeds doubt and fear. Action breeds confidence and courage. If you want to conquer fear, do not sit home and think about it. Go out and get busy." (Dale Carnegie.)[34]

"We will all experience one of two great pains in life. The pain of discipline or the pain of regret. The pain of discipline weighs ounces. The pain of regret weighs tons."

# CHAPTER 11

# If You Want It Done Right, Do It Yourself

## LEADERSHIP ILLUSION # 9

**T**he Effect: Nobody can accomplish that task better than you can so, if you want it done right, you're just going to have to do it yourself.

**The Secret:** This philosophy cripples and disables teams. It is also another form of ego that destroys confidence and trust in team members. Managers control people and tell them what to do. Leaders create other leaders who lead.

I almost titled this chapter "I'm Bossy, Therefore I'm a Good Leader." Both of these illusions deal with having a boss or manager's mindset versus having a leader's mindset. They're so closely intertwined that I decided to combine them into this one chapter.

Every physical therapist knows that if they do for their patient what the patient should be doing for themselves, it doesn't help them; it only hurts the patient in the long run. Every nurse knows they cannot make a patient recover from a leg injury by walking for them. At some point, that patient will have to try to walk on his own to begin the healing process. Parents know that doing a child's homework for them isn't truly helping them. The child is not learning the material themselves and they won't be prepared to enter the real world because they're not used to doing their own work.

They will end up with an entitlement mentality that everything should be given to them without them working for it.

These are a few prominent examples but, somehow, when applied to the area of a boss and leadership, this illusion is missed over and over again. The mentality of doing it yourself is nothing more than a veiled form of ego. It is the belief that nobody can do the job as well as you can; therefore, you should simply do it yourself. The downfall of this philosophy is that not only do you run yourself ragged by doing everything yourself but you also alienate the other team members by taking over their responsibilities. You also ultimately cripple them and prevent them from learning how to do things on their own. Remember, "Management is doing things right; leadership is doing the right things." (Peter Drucker.)[35]

Jeanette (not her real name) was an up-and-comer. She was sharply dressed, smart, and a serious-minded hard worker. She worked at a corporation with about 100 employees. Although she started in an administrative assistant position, upper management quickly took notice of her abilities—and what top management missed, Jeanette made sure she told them about. She was a bit of a self-promoter but she backed up everything she said with extreme action. She was a workaholic. She was very popular at the corporation and everyone appreciated her working hard to make it a better place.

> "Management is doing things right; leadership is doing the right things."

But as she moved into more significant leadership roles, things began to change. At first, it was very subtle. Only a few astute people noticed it. Eventually, it would be too big to miss. She began to exhibit a bossy attitude. She had told the stories many times of how her classmates in elementary school had said she was a bossy kid and, when her own child exhibited the same qualities, she found it endearing. She was pretty much the only one who did.

Instead of talking to people as she used to, once she acquired her new title, she began barking orders at people. Behind her back, she became known as "The Boss," and it wasn't meant as a kind thing. People became irritated with her words, and most of the employees felt as if she treated them like she was better than they were. She would often question those under her authority as to whether they were completing their work. She was constantly looking over their shoulders. It was a source of frustration for those who worked with her because they felt as if she thought they were incapable of doing their work without her constant nagging instructions. They felt as if she was always second-guessing everyone's work, as if she was an overbearing mother figure.

But it wasn't just her words. She also had the habit of doing people's jobs for them. When someone would ask for clarification about a given task, she would reply, "Just let me do it." And then she would! But when her supervisors asked if a job was completed, she also took credit for it. She was taking over other people's jobs. When she was occasionally confronted about it, she would apologize, then say, "I'm only trying to help get the job done." Deep down, she likely believed it was much easier and safer for her to do the job than to wait on the other person to do it. After all, what if they didn't follow through like they were supposed to?

She became known for overstepping her boundaries and being a micromanager. Some of the team members complained, especially the ones from whom she took responsibilities. They lived in fear of losing their jobs because somebody else had stepped in and begun doing their job. But her supervisors were simply looking at the bottom line: Was the job being done? She not only received credit for all those jobs being done, but she also received another promotion.

And then something inexplicable happened: Not only did she continue overstepping her authority and boundaries through her micromanagement techniques with those under her, but she began doing the same thing to some of the people in different departments. She had no authority there, but she wanted to help them "do things the right way," so she would boss around the support positions and often create confusion by doing so. The way the team members saw it was that when a member of the executive team told them what to do, they felt they had no choice but to do it, even when it conflicted with instructions from their immediate supervisor.

Her activities created chaos in some departments and more than a few confrontations with her peers, who were frustrated by her telling people in their departments how to do their jobs. She would simply deflect and tell them, "I'm just trying to help everyone do things more efficiently. I would think you would appreciate the help!" Only, they didn't.

Her other habit at this level was to go to an executive and tell them her opinions about how her peers in other departments weren't efficiently doing their jobs. And while some of her ideas and opinions held weight, her breach of protocol was massive. She rarely approached her peers to offer ideas. She simply went around, above, or below them to push her own agenda of "how things should be," leaving a trail of resentment in her wake.

Many of the employees and team members couldn't understand why the president of the company consistently allowed her to overstep her boundaries and interfere with others. And yet, he did. He likely felt that as long as the work was getting done and the profit margins were up, it didn't matter who had handled things. And so she gleefully continued her micromanaging, boundary-crossing ways.

The straw that broke the camel's back for her peer leaders was when Jeanette began handing out checklists for each department chair to complete and return to her on a weekly basis. She wasn't even the supervisor of some of them, but the president let her do it, saying, "It will probably help the productivity of each department." The first to leave were two on the executive team who were tired of her interference and the lack of leadership from the top. They moved to other companies, occupying similar positions for more money. The next to leave were those in the middle-management positions who couldn't stand being treated like kindergartners all of the time. By the time the president acknowledged that there was a problem with Jeanette, it was too late. Many of the good leaders had left, and he was left to deal with the monster that his own inaction had created.

He confronted Jeanette, but when she returned to her "I'm just trying to make this place run correctly" rhetoric, he realized how big the problem truly was. When he finally let her go, it was like a nuclear explosion in his company. The damage it caused took more than five years to recover from. By then, the company had not only lost a lot of good team members, but also a great deal of revenue.

Simply put: Micromanagement kills teams.

Often, "bossy" people or "loud" people are mistaken for leaders. Bossy people aren't leaders. In fact, they're almost always the most irritating people in the organization. As John Wayne aptly said in the movie *The Cowboys*, "A big mouth don't make a big man."

The easiest way to spot a boss versus a true leader is to look at their location. Bosses will nearly always be behind the group, telling them (often loudly) what to do. Think of them as the person in the back seat on a long trip who is continually yelling out directions or driving advice for the person in the driver's seat. Not fun! A leader, however, will be out in front of the team, showing them what to do and empowering them to do it on their own.

A micromanager will scrutinize and criticize and then often take over and do the job for someone. This would be the same thing as a parent who does all of their child's homework for them and then wonders why their child fails their tests in school (when the parent isn't there to do the work for them). Homework is designed for the child to learn

and do at home so they are prepared to answer things outside of the classroom. A parent who does all of the work for them isn't helping them; they're crippling them and creating an entitlement mentality.

Micromanagers and bosses can kill organizations quicker than anything.

I've had many people ask me about bosses and leaders, "Aren't they really the same thing?" The short answer is "No." Can a boss be a leader? Absolutely. It's all in the way they handle things and if they're open to personally growing. In truth, we need fewer managers and fewer bosses and a *lot* more leaders. Let's take a look at the differences.

> **Micromanagement kills teams.**

Here are some differences between managers and leaders:

| Managers | Leaders |
| --- | --- |
| Focus on tasks. | Focus on the overall vision. |
| Do things right. | Do the right things. |
| Plan. | Inspire. |
| Follow and enforce rules. | Make and break the rules occasionally. |
| Go with the flow. | Swim upstream. |
| Organize. | Influence. |
| Direct. | Motivate. |
| Lead through control. | Lead through building up others. |
| Drive an employee. | Coach them and build them up. |
| Lead from their position. | Lead from their influence. |
| Control others through fear. | Inspire trust in others. |
| Talk a lot using "I." | Use "we" a lot. |
| Use the blame game often. | Take ownership and fix the problem. |
| Know how things are done. | Have actually done it and so can show how it is done, or else will empower others who are more proficient in that task to do it. |
| Use people. | Develop people. |
| Take credit. | Give credit. |
| Boss people around. | Ask lots of questions. |
| Tell others what to do. | Say, "Let's do it." |

Remember, "Managers light a fire under people. Leaders light a fire in people." (Kathy Austin.)[36]

In nearly every organization, there will be a manager/boss. To a large degree, they are necessary to get some tasks done. However, a company or organization that is looking for a recipe for disaster is one that puts a manager/boss into a significant leadership position. This can demotivate teams and cause the real leaders to exit for a place that fosters freedom and synergy.

If you've read through this chapter, you have probably started identifying someone with these characteristics. If, by chance, you've seen some of these characteristics in yourself, don't fret. A boss and/or manager can become a leader. There just needs to be a shift in your thinking.

Here are a few practical suggestions:

1) **Listen more and say less.** The more you listen, the more you learn—and the more you connect. The goal is first to understand someone and then, after that, to be understood. Employing this one technique can help the vast majority of a person's leadership skills.

2) **Ask questions more than you give directives.** Henry Ford said, "A bore is a person who opens his mouth and puts his feats in."[37] It is essential, as leaders, to remember that nobody is interested in what *we* say or think. They are, however, very interested in what *they* say or think, and when we ask them about it, it shows that we value them. Form a consensus by getting the input of your team and organization. The more they know you value their opinions, the more "buy-in" your team will have and the more they'll feel a part of the overall vision.

3) **Never scold someone in public.** As a leader, you may have to correct someone's behavior, but keep in mind that they are a human being with feelings, just like you. Nobody wants to be publicly humiliated. Pull them aside privately. Always remember the principle of boiling water: Before you turn the heat up in the pot, always put the water in first; otherwise,

you'll scald the pot. The "water" you pour into a person is the positive things you say before and after you tell them something difficult or bring them some sort of correction. Always pour the water in first. After that, turn up the heat.

4) **Give credit to the team for victories.** Take ownership of the losses. Legendary University of Alabama coach Paul "Bear" Bryant was famous for saying that when Alabama won a football game, "It was an incredible team effort. These are good boys who worked hard." When Alabama lost, he would say, "It was bad coaching." The more credit you give to your team, the better leader you become. When things go wrong, if you, as the leader, own it and fix it, your team will be well on the way to success, and you will be on the road to authentic leadership.

5) **Actively look for and mentor others to do what you're doing.** I know that may sound scary to some people who may be insecure and fear that if they do that then someone else will take their position, but that's small thinking. That's a scarcity mentality. Real leaders have an abundance mentality and know that there is plenty of room for everyone. They also know that, in training and mentoring others, they are multiplying themselves and multiplying their own influence. Make it about other people's growth and successes.

6) **Never ask anyone to do something you yourself haven't done or aren't willing to do.** This one is huge in building team morale as well as building influence. People don't respect people who tell them to do something they haven't done or won't do. In fact, that is very close to the textbook definition of a hypocrite. If you lead by example instead of by words, you will have respect and greater influence with your team.

7) **Don't do the work for them!** Leading by example does not mean you're doing the work for them. You're teaching. You're instructing. You're leading by example. The actual

implementation must be by that person. They have to learn to do it on their own. Don't be that parent who cripples their child by doing all their homework for them. Teach them and empower them to do it on their own. Give them the freedom to fall down and learn from their mistakes—which brings me to the last point ...

8) **Make risk and failure the norm and provide a safe environment for it.** When you mentor and pour into people, they're going to fail. It's just part of it. If you're a leader then you know all too well that you have failed many times in your journey too. I'll talk more about that in a later chapter, but for now it is up to you as the leader to allow those you influence to be able to fail—and not fear they'll lose their job because they took a chance on something or didn't do something as well as someone else. I'm not talking about large moral failures here either; I'm talking about the freedom to try something that has never been attempted before and fall flat on your face in the process. The key is for that person to be able to learn and grow from their mistakes and become better. That happens with the guidance of a mentor and a leader. Your constructive input into someone's life and your grace and instruction for them when they mess up can be the keys to take their leadership to a new level that will surpass anything they previously thought possible. And when they arrive at that level, they'll have you to thank. That's what leaders do.

> "Managers light a fire under people. Leaders light a fire in people."

Remember, "I measure my own success as a leader by how well the people who work for me succeed." (Maria Shi.)[38]

The book *Band of Brothers*, written by noted historical novelist Stephen Ambrose, details the true stories of the US Army's 506th division during World War II. There is one particular part of this story (it was also an award-winning HBO miniseries) that clearly illustrates this particular leadership illusion. One of the people talked about in the book is Richard Winters. He started out in boot camp in Toccoa, Georgia, with the rest of the 506th and, through his influence, quickly distinguished himself as a leader both with the men and those in leadership above him. He overcame the "boss" mentality of a cruel leader named Herbert Sobel. Sobel was a very organized and capable officer, but he led the men through fear, intimidation, cruel over-discipline, and blaming others for his own mistakes. Sobel was an inept, ineffective battlefield leader. He made numerous mistakes during military exercises that led the men in his charge not to trust him in battle when their lives were on the line.

Sobel regularly punished Winters for Sobel's own mistakes. When he falsely accused Winters of something he didn't do, Winters refused to sign his disciplinary form and requested a formal hearing. This event led to Sobel being promoted out of the 506th and Winters eventually rising as their leader. Yes, you read that right: They promoted Sobel and moved him into a supply job that suited his more detail-obsessed nature.

Winters led his paratroopers into the frontlines of D-Day on June 6, 1944, firing his rifle and risking his own life bravely in the service of his country. In charging another small town, Winters was promoted to a higher leadership position and led his men with his rifle in hand at the front of the line, storming an entire German SS regiment. He led from the front, never from the rear. He never told anyone what to do; he showed them.

He was promoted to major over the entire 506th Division, and Captain Norman Dike took Winters's position. Known as "Foxhole Norman," Dike was infamous for staying at the back of the lines and even leaving his men on the battlefield during the Battle of the Bulge, one of the most infamous and bloody battles of World War II. Winters stayed with his men regardless.

After the Battle of the Bulge, when the time came, Dike was supposed to lead the charge against the village of Foy, Belgium, which was filled with Germans. He froze. When the time came for true leadership, he couldn't make a decision. The men began to die due to his lack of leadership. Winters relieved him and sent Captain Ronald Speirs to replace him. Captain Speirs led them to victory that day, again—by example—from the front.

Major Richard Winters exemplified true leadership. He led by example. He didn't tell the men what to do; he showed them. He never asked them to do anything he wasn't willing to do himself. But he also didn't do for the men what they should have been doing for themselves. He empowered them to become great soldiers and effective leaders. He came into that position prepared and ready, and the men saw this. He liberally gave credit to others for their battlefield heroism. He showed compassion while maintaining discipline. He never led through fear; he consistently inspired trust.

I realize this has been one of the longest chapters in the book, but rightfully so. This one illusion trips up more organizations than just about any other I've seen. If you've been a manager, abandon that mentality. Go back and read the list of managers versus leaders and see where you fall. Make the necessary adjustments—starting today.

And remember, if you want things done right, show others, inspire others, lead others, create others who can do it, empower others to do it, let others do it on their own—even if they fail at first—and give others credit for it when it's finally done. That's what a true leader does. Remember, "The greatest leader is not necessarily the one who does the greatest things. He is the one who gets the people to do the greatest things." (Ronald Reagan.)[39]

He never led through fear;
he consistently inspired trust.

# CHAPTER 12

# AS A LEADER, I HAVE ALL THE ANSWERS AND AM NEVER WRONG

**The Effect:** A leader has to know more than everyone and have all of the answers to be qualified to lead, and they can never appear to their team to be wrong about anything.

**The Secret:** A true leader assembles experts around them in their own areas. A true leader knows that having others around them who are more talented, more knowledgeable, and more equipped raises the level of the entire organization.

I am a fan of the old *The Andy Griffith Show* for many reasons. I like that it is a show an entire family can watch together. I love the characters on the show. I'm a fan of character-driven comedies (like *The Andy Griffith Show, Seinfeld, Boston Legal,* etc.). Some of the characters are outlandish and hilarious to watch. Perhaps one of the funniest comedy characters of all time (in my opinion) was Barney Fife. Early on in the series, Andy tried to be funny. You can really see this played out in the first season. Andy quickly realized that his job was to play the straight man to everyone else's zany characters. It worked. The chemistry between Andy and Barney was pure magic. Andy was mainly the mature, wise one and Barney was just a big kid. It was fun to watch him react to various situations.

Some of his funniest moments occurred when he was asked a question he didn't know the answer to and would attempt to seem intelligent by giving a faux answer. Some of those answers were doozies! Here are a few of my favorites:

- "Do you know how old Albert Einsteen was when he graduated?" (It's Albert Ein*stein*.)

- "Those are your true schizophreeneeacs!" (It's schizo*phrenic*.)

- "It's the old mother figure bit! Sigmund Frood wrote a lot about that!" (It's Sigmund *Freud*.)

- "ESP! You know: People on mountains miles apart thinking the same thoughts ... you know: extra-sensitive perception." (It's extra*sensory* perception.)

- "We gotta get some guy that hasn't been around a lot. You know, somebody really nave." (It's *naïve*.)

- "We don't have a radio dispatcher, nor a crime lab, nor a fingerprint filer, or a teletype machine, or a radar ... We don't even have a heeliocopter!" (It's *heli*copter.)

- "I was an avaricious reader." (It's a *voracious* reader. Avaricious refers to a person who is greedy and materialistic.)

My all-time favorite of Barney's is when he was lecturing a group of boys on the dangers of ending up in prison:

Barney: "This is where our most incorrigible prisoners are incarcerated. The idea of being incarcerated scares you, doesn't it?"

Opie: "Yeah! And we don't even know what it means!"

Another boy jumps in: "I know what it means! It's like when a doctor gives you a shot."

Barney smiles: "No son. That's *inarculated*." (It's *inocu*lated.)

Barney makes me laugh. It's his complete confidence in what he thinks he knows but actually doesn't.

Now, that's all well and good for a comedy TV show but, in leadership, that's a bad thing. Ronald Reagan once said about his political critics, "It's not that they're ignorant. It's that they know so much that isn't so."[40]

There are a couple of questions that must be answered for us to overcome this leadership illusion and bring it into the light. The first question is, what do you not know?

This must be answered with brutal honesty. There is nothing worse in leadership than a leader who is acting as if he knows it all in an attempt to fool those around him. Here's the truth: He isn't fooling anybody. Neither are you. If you don't know something, the best thing you can do is admit it.

> "It's not that they're ignorant. It's that they know so much that isn't so."

My father was a classically trained musician, but he was raised on a rural farm in Missouri. It was there he learned how to plant, cultivate, and, eventually, harvest. He kept that love of growing things throughout his life. When I was growing up, during the spring and summer our entire backyard in the city where I was raised was almost always tilled soil full of plants growing. My particular favorites were the homegrown tomatoes. I don't know why homegrown tomatoes tasted so much better than store-bought ones, but they did then and they still do now. Most of you know that tomatoes grow green and then eventually turn red. As a young boy, when I was helping my dad in the garden, I would sometimes want to pick the tomatoes too early, and Dad would remind me, "No, son. That's green. Leave it alone."

One day we were in his garden, Dad pointed to a tomato and said, "Go ahead and pick that one." I looked at it, and there were some green streaks on a side he couldn't see. I said, "No, Dad. This one still has some green on it." He replied, "No. That one's ripe enough. Go ahead and take it." And then he said something I've never forgotten: "When it's green, it's growing, but when it's ripe, it's next to rotten. The same thing is true of you. Never think you know it all. Always be in a state of learning. Always be in a state of growth."

If you don't know something, that's perfectly fine. If you're in a state of personal growth at all times, you'll never be at that "rotten" moment where you think you've "arrived" and have no further need of knowledge.

The second question is an incredibly important one: *Who* do you know? Most people spend their time contemplating *how* they can do something or *how* they can learn it, when the best question is actually *who* they know who can already do that thing proficiently.

Here's the truth: There are some things you do that you're a "ten" at. You're at the top of your game when you're doing them. But there are some things in which your absolute best efforts will yield a result of a three or four. And if you work extra hard in that area, focus on it, and develop it, then you might get to be a six or seven in that area. That's a positive, right?

No. It isn't.

> Never think you know it all.
> Always be in a state of learning.

When you begin to focus your energy on developing that weakness, your strength begins to suffer. What you did as a ten now drops to an eight, a seven, or even a six. There are people out there who are tens in your four-to-five area. You probably despise doing the job that yields a result of a four or six for you, but they would absolutely be thrilled to do it, and they're already a ten at it! Now, instead of having one person working at a seven or eight in their strength and a four or five in their weakness, you now have two people working at level ten in their strengths.

My dad was great at fixing things. He thrived on it. He would visit my house, bring his tool kit, and, by the time he left, every single thing in my house that wasn't working at 100 percent would be there by the time he left. Somehow, that gene skipped a generation. I'm terrible at fixing or constructing things. It never goes right for me. Things that are supposed to be straight are always crooked. When I build things from a box store, there are still parts left over that shouldn't be there. It's a nightmare. As a builder, I'm easily a two or three. I have friends who are tens at building things.

So, I still fix things. I just fix them with a checkbook instead of my hands. That is a better use of my talent and abilities.

Recently, one of my builder friends needed help drafting an important letter for his business. He's a three or four in writing. I gladly wrote the letter for him. In writing, I'm easily a nine or ten. It just flows for me. He was happy, and so was I.

The next time a challenge arises that you don't know how to solve, don't ask, "How?" Instead, ask, "Who?"

Here are a few more keys in this area that have helped me:

1) Stay humble! Nobody knows it all. The good news is you don't ever have to know it all. You simply need to find people who *do* know what you need. Be willing to acknowledge what you don't know. Remember, most of your team is already aware of the fact that you don't know it anyway. The best thing to do is acknowledge it.

2) Get to know experts in other fields that could help shore up your weaknesses. Add value to them in areas of their

weakness and empower them to help you in your areas of need.

3) Keep the relationships with those experts strong. It is crucial to empower them to do what they do best and not attempt to micromanage them, as we discussed in the last chapter.

4) When something goes right, be sure to spread the credit for the victory to your team members. Remember, "A man may do an immense deal of good, if he does not care who gets the credit for it." (Father Strickland.)[41]

5) When something goes wrong, take the blame. Taking responsibility not only creates trust in your leadership, but also empowers you to develop solutions for the problem. It also forces us to look at the only person we can truly fix: ourselves!

> ## Don't ask, "How?"
> ## Instead, ask, "Who?"

Remember, "If you could kick the person in the pants responsible for most of your trouble, you wouldn't sit for a month." (Theodore Roosevelt.)[42]

Henry Ford was once criticized for not personally knowing how to build a car. He simply replied, "I don't have to know how to build a car. I just have to know people who know how to build them." Keep that in mind. You don't have to know it all. You simply have to know people who fill in the gaps in your areas of weakness and then use *your* strengths to fill in *their* weaknesses. That's a great team! Empower others to shine through exercising their strengths and praise them and give them credit for it. Do that, and you'll be well on your way to being a great team leader who earns the respect of their entire team.

# CHAPTER 13

# BETTER SAFE THAN SORRY!

**T**he Effect: Better safe than sorry! You don't need to take risks. Play it safe!

**The Secret:** There are no rewards, nor is there any sort of significant progress made, without taking risks. It is just part of leadership and success. Playing it safe all of the time is a sure road to mediocrity.

If you were to look at Dan, you wouldn't see anything exceptional about him. He was only about 5'7". He came from a lower-middle-class family. It was a very large family of fourteen kids. He was in the middle of that pack. None of his siblings had ever gone to college. They were very blue-collar—not that there's anything wrong with any of that, but Dan had a dream: Dan wanted to play collegiate football. He didn't have much athletic ability at all. He wasn't an academic standout either, barely making passing grades in high school. He was considered slow by some of his teachers. His family members weren't encouraging either, telling him to get his head out of the clouds and back to reality. After all, none of his family members had made it to college. Why should he?

But Dan was determined. The death of one of his closest friends and encouragers in his life spurred him to go after his dream. So he packed his things and moved. His dream wasn't to play collegiate football just anywhere; he only wanted to play at one school: Notre Dame. And at that time, Notre Dame was one of the top collegiate football programs in the nation. Notre Dame was also one of the toughest academic schools to get into, so the deck was stacked against him.

Realizing his grades weren't good enough for him to get into Notre Dame, Daniel "Rudy" Ruettiger moved to South Bend and attended a nearby junior college. He'd been diagnosed with dyslexia. Once he knew and understood more about his disability, he was able to conquer it and make good grades. After applying to Notre Dame and being turned down multiple times, he was finally accepted to the school, surprising his parents and family members.

The next step was trying out for the Notre Dame football team. Ninety-five players received full-ride scholarships to Notre Dame. Fifteen others also tried out. Rudy was one of those. The NCAA regulations only allowed them to dress sixty players for their home games. Rudy had no scholarship and very little athletic ability but, what he lacked in athletic ability, he made up for with his heart. He had an indefatigable spirit that inspired and challenged those around him.

He made the practice team. He served in that capacity for two years, taking beating after beating from the starters in every practice. His heart was always to make the team better. In his last home game, Rudy earned the right to be one of the sixty starters who ran out on the field as a football player for Notre Dame. Not only that, but the coach let him play in the final minutes of that game versus Georgia Tech in 1975. On the last play of that game, with five seconds left, Rudy sacked the Georgia Tech quarterback, officially putting his name forever in the record book of Notre Dame football. The other players lifted Rudy on their shoulders and carried him off the field that day.

Just to recap:

- He was too small and nonathletic to play football.
- He didn't have the background, money, or grades to get into Notre Dame.
- He had dyslexia.
- He should never have overcome his learning disability to make good grades, but he did.
- He should never have gotten into Notre Dame academically or financially, but he did.
- He should never have made the Notre Dame football team over the scholarship players, but he did.
- He should never have been able to dress for a Notre Dame football game, but he did.
- He should never have been put on the field for the game, but he was.
- He should never have been able to sack the opposing quarterback in the game, but he did.
- He should never have been carried off the field, but he remains the only player in Notre Dame football history ever to be carried off the field.

Rudy was quoted as saying, "The power of a dream is giving someone hope."[43] That is the power of a dream. That is the power of taking a risk. If you want to achieve great things, you have to take risks and pursue your dream with all of your heart.

> "The power of a dream is giving someone hope."

I was sitting in a large seminar. The gentleman on stage was motivational speaker and pastor Dr. Robert Schuller. He posed a question that has stayed with me: "What would you attempt if you knew you couldn't fail?" It was a powerful question that brought several things in my life into focus. I realized that much of what was holding me back from fulfilling my own potential was based on an illusion, a lie.

> "What would you attempt if you knew you couldn't fail?"

One of Yogi Berra's famously funny quotes applies here. "Ninety percent of the putts that are short don't go in."[44] We, as a society, are risk-avoidant. We shy away from risk. But anyone who has ever achieved any measure of great success has had to take a risk—a leap of faith, if you will. After I listened to Dr. Schuller's message, I wrote down a few questions for myself and had a time of self-reflection. Here are my questions:

1) **What is your biggest dream?** I'm not talking about some sweet little dream. I mean what Jim Collins in his book *Good to Great* calls "a big, hairy, audacious goal (BHAG)." It's that dream that cannot be accomplished through any natural means of your own. It would take the entire universe conspiring for you to achieve it. It's that thing that you won't tell anybody because it seems so outrageous and ridiculous, and you know they'll make fun of you for even entertaining the idea. That's the dream I'm talking about. Have you written it down? If not, stop and do it right now. Don't read any more until you do it. Seriously—do it now.

2) **What happens if this dream doesn't come true?** I have a friend who was talking to me about pursuing a law degree. It has always been his dream to be a lawyer. When he spoke to me about it, his face lit up and there was a fire in his eyes. You could just tell this was his real purpose and his dream. But he also had family members questioning whether he was smart enough to complete the degree and pass the bar exam. Nobody in their family had accomplished such a task. Then he said this to me: "I just don't know. It's going to take me four years of hard study to do this, and I'm not sure the time is right. I mean, I'm forty years old. I'll be forty-four when I complete it." I looked at him and asked him the same question I had asked myself above: "What happens if you don't do it?" He just looked at me. I continued, "If you don't do it, in four years you're still going to be forty-four years old. Right?" A light bulb went off, and he realized that pursuing his dream was a much better option than doing nothing. If he failed or didn't complete it, time would still pass, and he'd still be right where he was today. Today, my friend is fifty years old and a lawyer with a very successful practice. He took the risk, pursued his dream, and accomplished his goal, and he is loving his life!

3) **What happens if this dream does come true?** Think of all of the possibilities that will happen for you if it *does* come true. Actually write them down. What type of life will you be living? Who will you be helping? Where will you be living? How will your life and the lives of others be changed and impacted? Write all of these things down. Go ahead and do it now before you go on. Take some time here. Now that you've written it down, look at what you just wrote. Weigh those things you've written down against those fears and insecurities holding you back. In ten years, you're going to be ten years older whether you accomplish these things or not. But with some self-discipline and focus, your life in ten years can look vastly different than it does today. It's all in your hands right now!

**4) What calculated risk can you take?** There is a vast difference in an unreasonable risk and a *calculated* risk. Jumping out of an airplane is risky. Jumping out of an airplane with no parachute is stupid. Jumping out of an airplane in tandem with an experienced, certified skydiver is a calculated risk. Of course there is some risk, but it is greatly minimized by taking some precautions and by going through it with someone with experience. The same is true of the risks we take in life in our business and professions. Is there anyone who has already accomplished what you're wanting to do? Get with them! Ask to be mentored by them. Learn from them! I have used this technique over and over to learn new things. Mentors can show you how to take steps toward your dream while avoiding the large "land mines" on your road. They've walked the pathway already. They know where the major pitfalls are. They can help you! Even if you have to pay for them (which, most of the time, you do), it's *so* worth it to learn from them. Are there classes or seminars on what you're wanting to do? Invest in them and learn something from people who have walked your road. Read a book on the subject. There are all sorts of ways to learn to move a huge risk into the "calculated risk" category. Doing this will move you closer to your big dream.

**5) What is one step you can take toward that goal this week?** Write it down. Add it to your "to-do" list. Again, don't wait. Do it now. Every person with a dream has taken risks to see that dream come true. Walt Disney mortgaged his house multiple times in order to finance his dreams on film and, eventually, in the Disney parks. Numerous successful actors in Hollywood started out by leaving their hometowns, moving to Hollywood, and suffering through poverty and menial minimum-wage jobs while going to multiple auditions every week until their big breaks came. Harrison Ford struggled in Hollywood as a painter and construction worker until his big break came in George

Lucas's film *American Graffiti*. That film led to Harrison landing the role of Han Solo and, eventually, Indiana Jones. He was thirty-five years old when he played Han Solo and had been struggling in Hollywood for years. Most people would have given up. He didn't. Today, he is still one of the highest-paid, most successful actors in Hollywood. But he suffered through years of failure and risk-taking to get to his goal. Every one of us has to be willing to take those risks. Some will pay off. Many will not. But that's part of it. There is another definition of "risk," and it is called "faith." Faith believes things to be there and tangible and real before they actually are. My favorite book defines faith this way: "Faith is the substance of things hoped for. The evidence of things not seen."[45] In the movie *Indiana Jones and the Last Crusade*, Harrison Ford perfectly acts out what this chapter is about. He has to take both a literal and figurative leap of faith from the lion's head in order to find the treasured Holy Grail. He has to put his foot forward and take a step without seeing any sort of support below him. Of course, he does it and finds there is an invisible support there that leads to the treasure. How appropriate is it for Harrison Ford to be acting out in that movie what the first part of his life embodied?

Our treasured dreams are waiting for us beyond the leap of faith. I encourage you today to take that step. You may not be able to see what is in front of you. Take the step anyway. You may fall on your face. That's okay too. Just get up and take another step. Keep going. Your dreams are worth it. So are you.

Take another step. Keep going.
Your dreams are worth it.
So are you.

# CHAPTER 14

# WHAT YOU DON'T KNOW
# WON'T HURT YOU

LEADERSHIP ILLUSION # 12

**T**he Effect: Ignorance is bliss. What you don't know won't hurt you.

**The Secret:** What you don't know can bite you—*hard.* Details often make or break you.

I love the old *Far Side* cartoons. I love the quirky humor and slice-of-life observations. As a musician, one of my favorite ones featured a guy in an orchestra. His job was to crash the cymbals. However, he was only holding one cymbal in one hand, and his other hand was empty. (If you're not musical, he's supposed to be holding one cymbal in each hand to crash them together.) You can see the guy concentrating and saying to himself, "This time, I won't screw up! I won't! I won't! I won't! I won't!" The caption reads, "Roger screws up."

Okay, me describing it is not nearly as funny as you seeing the visual, but you get the idea. Missing a detail like holding two cymbals instead of one will make for a pitiful cymbal crash.

Have you ever gone on a mission to shop at a store for something and gotten up to the counter to pay, only to realize you didn't bring your money or credit cards with you? I have. I've done the same thing in a drive-through after I've ordered my food! I've witnessed people in the airport trying to board flights without their passport or driver's licenses because they forgot them. Then there was a pastor friend of mine who was baptizing people in the baptistry at the beginning of the service before he preached. He had plenty of time to change clothes while the music was going on, and he had brought other clothes to wear—with one exception: He'd forgotten his underwear. So his choices were to wear wet underwear under his new clothes or to go "commando." He ended up wearing the wet underwear, but he went to the choir room and borrowed a choir robe to preach in.

> ## Hire your weaknesses and delegate so the details are covered.

Forgetting little details can make for some embarrassing situations! It can also make for some disasters. Jack was an extremely dedicated worker. He knew his job and worked hard at it. His main job was to transmit messages from ship to shore. The previous day, the system was down, so he had a backlog of personal messages to be sent, which he was diligently doing. He had gotten through all of them but had accidentally let two of them slip through the cracks. Those messages were to be sent to Cape Race, Newfoundland, and Jack determined to get them done. It was priority number one. So you can imagine his irritation when another ship sent him a weather message. Seeing that message as not nearly as important as getting those personal messages through, Jack chose to table the message, not reporting it to the bridge, and continued trying to send his messages through.

Evans was also dedicated to his work. He worked on a ship that was near Jack. Evans saw his own vessel in danger due to the weather and got them to stop. He sent a message to Jack's ship, warning him of impending problems on the sea. He got a message back from Jack that said, "Keep out. Shut up. I'm working Cape Race." Evans chose to see if there were any more messages from Jack, but there weren't, so he turned off his radio equipment and went to sleep.

A little while later, Evans woke up and saw some bursts in the sky off in the distance. He awakened his captain to view the phenomenon too. The captain told him to ignore it and go back to sleep, so Evans did. What neither of them knew at that time—12:47 a.m. on April 15, 1912—is that those crewman aboard the *Californian* were visually witnessing the sinking of HMS *Titanic*. Evans could have known it, but he had turned his radio off after Jack had told him to shut up.

And John "Jack" Phillips? He was the radio operator aboard the *Titanic*, diligently sending those messages to Cape Race, Newfoundland. The message he ignored and didn't take to his bridge: "Icebergs blocking the path." The message from Evans? "Our ship is surrounded by ice!" Jack received separate warnings from two different ships and chose to ignore them, leading to one of the biggest disasters in history.

Small details can sink large ships.

Some people have a knack for details, but I'll just confess to you now: I'm not one of them. Many times in my life, little details have bitten me in the rear end. If you're in the same boat, don't fret. There are solutions. I'm going to give you a few that have helped me:

1) If you're not a detail-oriented person, find people who *are* detail-oriented and recruit them. Empower them to handle those details for you. Remember, as we discussed in a previous chapter, good leaders empower others to be leaders and operate in their strength zone. You can absolutely be a

leader and not be a detail-oriented person, as long as you have detail-oriented people around you to fill in that weakness.

2) Use mind maps. Mind-mapping has been around for a long time. I personally use a program from Mindjet to do mine. I've used this program for years. Basically, a mind map is where you sit down and map out every aspect of a project. When I started doing this twenty years ago, I would get a large 11" x 14" piece of paper and draw circles and lines on it, mapping out each section of my project. At first, it took me days and sometimes more than a week to map things out. I would forget important details and remember them at 3 a.m.! (Side note: I still keep a notepad on my nightstand for this very reason.) As I continued using this method, though, I got better and better at it, and the process would last a day or two instead of a week. Today, my entire team participates in the mind-mapping process, and it usually takes us only a few hours to map out an entire project. Teamwork is a critical concept in this type of planning, and having detail-oriented people on that team is critically important. The more "A" players you have on your team who are strong in their own areas of expertise, the less likely you'll be to miss vital details.

3) Once you have the project details mapped out, assign deadline dates to every line item and put them on a master calendar. I realize this process sounds tedious (it is) but it's necessary in order to avoid missing important details. Later on, when the project is in full swing and everyone's schedule is hectic from carrying out the work, you'll be glad you took this step. My personality style despises sitting down and doing detailed planning like this, but it is absolutely necessary, and the "pain" I feel for a few hours or days spent planning is nothing compared to the pain of missing important things and looking bad. There is no feeling like knowing you and your team have mapped out the possibilities and have your bases covered. You'll lift a huge

load from everyone's shoulders by going through with this type of planning.

4) Once you're sure you have all of the details planned out, show the entire project to more detail-oriented people (preferably from outside of your organization) to see if they see anything you've missed. An outsider with a fresh perspective can prove to be invaluable in this process.

5) Have a project manager follow up on the deadlines. If deadlines aren't being met then the mind map and the planning process aren't worth more than the paper they're printed on. The project manager shouldn't be a tyrant (or a boss!). They should simply be there for purposes of accountability. If some dates need to be changed, do it. The mind map isn't a binding legal document. It should be fluid with the rest of the team, and you'll find as you work together that some of the dates will change. Sitting down and planning out these details isn't a fun process for me, but I have team members who thrive on this type of activity. I mean, they love it! Look for people with that type of temperament for your team, and you'll have a strong group ready to face the details and succeed at whatever you can dream!

> ## Small details can sink large ships.

I once visited Israel and, while in Bethlehem, I visited the tomb of St. Jerome. It is located in a basement below the famous Church of the Nativity. St. Jerome is credited with translating the Bible from Hebrew into the Latin Vulgate. It was one of the most significant translations in the history of the Bible, which remains today the best-selling book of all time. But … it wasn't entirely without mistakes. One of the most notable ones had to do with St. Jerome's translation of a Hebrew word in the Old Testament. You see, Hebrew words don't contain vowels; they're merely inferred in context with the other words. The passage in question was from Exodus 34 and referred to the "krn of Moses." Correctly translated, it is *karan*, which means *radiance*. It was speaking of Moses's face being radiant and shining brightly. However, St. Jerome added some incorrect vowels to that word and translated it as *keren*, which actually means *horns*.

This led to legends that Moses actually had horns on his head. Surely, people knew that wasn't the case, right? Well … not exactly. In fact, that legend stuck so much that over 1,000 years later in the early 1500s, famous sculptor Michelangelo actually did a statue of Moses—with horns coming out of his head, based on St. Jerome's translation. That statue still exists today at the Vatican in Rome. Oops!

Little details matter! What you don't know can hurt you, others, and entire organizations. If you aren't a detail-oriented person, get people around you who are. Hire your weaknesses and delegate so the details are covered. Build a strong team. If you are a detailed-oriented person, volunteer your services to those who aren't. They have strengths you don't have and, together, you can be a formidable team.

As a leader, ignorance is never bliss. Ignorance is a ticking time bomb. The only way to diffuse that bomb is through handling the details or having a strong team that reliably handles the details. Whatever you do, don't ignore it!

Don't let your leader*ship* sink because of small details!

> Ignorance is a ticking time bomb.

# CHAPTER 15

# I Can't Be a Leader.
# I've Blown It.

**T**he Effect: "I've made huge mistakes. I've blown it. I can't be a leader!"

**The Secret**: There aren't any leaders who have experienced any significant level of success who haven't blown it—some of them in *major* ways. Perfection has never been a prerequisite for leadership. Learning from our mistakes and not repeating them is what qualifies us for true leadership.

Eli wanted to be a farmer. It wasn't much of a surprise, since his father was a farmer. When he started working, the farm part didn't work out, so he went to work for the railroad and helped build the Union Pacific Railroad that stretched to Colorado. While there, Eli became a professional fiddle player. He didn't make it. He tried working as a mailman in Kissimmee, Florida. He didn't make it doing that either.

He worked as a construction worker in Chicago, Illinois. That seemed to go well for him. He built and sold quite a few houses. He got married and had a few kids. But when he saw the rising crime in the area in which he lived, he decided to pursue his dream of having a farm again and moved his family to Missouri, where he bought a large farm. The town was a small, picturesque

American town. The farm he bought had pigs, chickens, horses, and cows, as well as crops.

He really tried to make it as a farmer but, ultimately, he couldn't do it. His older sons disliked the whole farming idea and moved back to Chicago. Eli's health began to fail and he had to sell the farm, after which he moved to Kansas City, Missouri. His sons who were still at home liked being in the big city. Eli and his son (also named Eli) had a large paper route. Rain or shine, snow or heat, young Eli was delivering papers for his father's route at 4 a.m. every morning.

Eli Sr. never made it as a farmer. He knew the sting of failure. So when young Eli told his father he had a dream of being an artist, his father was even more critical. Young Eli had been doodling on school papers since he was very young. He didn't like school at all and wanted to focus on being an artist. His father saw it as a useless distraction and one that couldn't make a penny, much less a living.

But young Eli was undaunted. He ended up becoming an artist for the local paper, but he knew there was only so much work for an artist in Kansas City, Missouri. He was considered difficult to work with, and his boss stole his ideas and took all of the credit for them. Young Eli was fired from that job and was broke and had no prospects for work. Just like his father, he had failed.

So he moved to California to live with his uncle. One of his brothers was also living there and working as a banker. Young Eli had finally decided that he needed to work for himself. He had an idea that would make his art unique and combined it (being in California) with movies. He worked hard on the concept and found a little bit of success. He also created an animated character of a rabbit that was moderately successful. Universal (the movie studio) took an interest in his character, and Eli was just on the cusp of making it big and showing his father that he could be a success as an artist. He had a meeting set up in New York with Universal but, when he got to the meeting, he was informed that Universal had taken many of the other artists and animators he had hired to work on his character and actually stolen the rights to his rabbit, named Oswald.

Once again—failure. Young Eli was left with no employees, no company, no character (that he had created!), and no money. Universal offered him a steady job with a salary, but Eli knew he couldn't work for anybody but himself.

One the way back to California, young Eli made a decision to keep going. He had learned from his mistakes. His mistakes had been costly and devastating. Most people would have given up and taken the security of a salary, but not Eli. He was determined to succeed. He pulled out a piece of paper and began scribbling a new character on it.

Eli Sr. was known to everyone as Elias. His son, young Eli, shared the same name as his middle name but was known to everyone by his first name: Walter—Walter Elias Disney. The character he drew on that piece of paper was Mortimer the Mouse, but his wife, Lillian, thought "Mortimer" was a terrible name and suggested the name "Mickey Mouse." And the rest is history.

It was through his failures that Walt learned about copyright protection, as well as marketing and franchising. He became an incredible entrepreneur, and his movies revolutionized the film industry and are still among the most beloved movies today. He also, of course, revolutionized theme parks, creating a clean, safe environment for families to play together, and those parks are visited by millions of people every year.

Later in life, Walt was quoted as saying, "I think it's important to have a good hard failure when you're young. I learned a lot out of that. Because it makes you kind of aware of what can happen to you. Because of it, I've never had any fear in my whole life when we've been near collapse and all of that. I've never been afraid. I've never had the feeling I couldn't walk out and get a job doing something."[46]

Many times when he was starting out, he mortgaged everything he had to fulfill his dream. First, it was for the first full-length animated movie ever created, *Snow White*. Critics told him nobody would sit for almost two hours to watch a cartoon. It made the Disney studio millions of dollars. Then it was for Disneyland. It started off rough, but Walt knew he had a winner of an idea.

Walt failed and failed again. It seemed to be a pattern from his father, but he never let those failures define him. He knew that failure was an occurrence, not a destination. He learned the lessons from each one and saw them as opportunities to move forward into his destiny.

Failure is inevitable for a successful person. The only question is, what will you do with the failure? Will you let it define you or let it propel you forward? The biggest issue with failing is psychologically overcoming the pain of it. We usually are our own worst critics, and we tend to be the hardest on ourselves. Legendary coach John Wooden said, "If you are afraid to fail, you will never do the things you are capable of doing."[47]

> What will you do with the failure? Will you let it define you or let it propel you forward?

Here are a few practical steps that have helped me and others in this area:

1) If you've blown it, admit it. The truth is that your team and organization probably already know it. The absolute worst thing you can do is pretend it didn't happen, lie about it, or ignore it. The best thing you can do is admit it, acknowledge it, and take the proper steps to see that it doesn't happen again. If there are consequences of your mistake or failure, embrace them, learn from them, and move on. Don't wallow in them. How do you do that?

2) Get two sheets of paper and number them at the top "1" and "2."

3) On sheet "1," write out the mistakes you've made. They can be the ones you've made at work or in your personal life: emotional, financial, physical, professional … whatever they are, write them on sheet 1. Be honest about it. Nobody is ever going to see this sheet but you. If you need extra paper (I get it!) then get it. Write them all out. Number them.

4) On sheet "2," begin to write out what you learned from each failure. Number them. Take your time. Really think about each one. Write down every single thing you can think of about what you learned. This may take you a few days. If that's the case, that's fine. Take the time.

5) Once you've written down everything you've learned on sheet 2, read it out loud: every lesson, every learning experience.

6) Take sheet 1 and *burn it*. Shred it. Get rid of it. Too many times, we spend our lives focusing on sheet 1 and ignoring sheet 2. Sheet 2 is where the value is. Sheet 1 does us no good. There isn't one thing we can do about mistakes or past failures except *learn* from them. Learn from your mistakes. Better yet, read and study and learn from *other people's* mistakes! I like to say it this way: "A wise person learns from their mistakes. A genius learns from somebody else's!" Motivational speaker Jim Rohn suggested interviewing

successful and not-so-successful people and learning from their wins and losses. That's valuable information for you to learn from. Dr. John C. Maxwell said, "Experience isn't the best teacher. If it were, then the wisest people in the world would be in the nursing homes across the world. It's not what we experience that causes us to grow. It's what we learn from it. So experience isn't the best teacher. Evaluated experience is the best teacher."[48]

7) Take sheet 2 and keep it in a place where you'll see it. Mine are usually on my bathroom mirror. Continually remind yourself of what you've learned and how you've grown.

8) Realize that every person who has had any sort of significant success has had to walk through the path of failure to get there:

a) **Thomas Edison** was called "too stupid to learn anything" by one of his teachers. He was fired from his first two jobs for being unproductive. When he failed at making the light bulb over 1,000 times and a reporter asked him how it felt to fail 1,000 times, Edison simply replied, "I didn't fail 1,000 times. The light bulb was an invention with 1,000 steps."[49]

b) **Abraham Lincoln** started in the army as a captain in the Black Hawk War but came home a private. When he entered politics, he won a few elections, but he also lost quite a few. He failed to get the nomination to be a senator from Illinois—twice. And, in 1860, he was elected as the sixteenth president of the United States of America, and is still considered one of the greatest leaders in the history of the United States.[50]

c) **Rowland** opened four retails stores in twelve years that all failed. He learned from his mistakes and kept going until, in 1858, he moved to New York City. There, Rowland Hussey Macy opened Macy's Department Store. To this day, it remains one of the most successful retail stores of all time.[51]

d) **Winston Churchill** suffered defeat and lost his position in the government during World War I. He was defeated when he ran for Parliament. And yet he became one of the most powerful and prominent leaders in Britain during World War II and saved Europe (along with the Allies) from a takeover by the Nazis.[52]

e) **Babe Ruth** was famous for his home-run record, but he also held the record for the most strikeouts! He used to say, "Every strike brings me closer to my next home run."[53]

f) My favorite book describes a guy named **Simon Peter** who shot his mouth off continuously. He was a close follower of Jesus and bragged about how, though others might leave, he would follow Jesus to the death. But when push came to shove and Jesus was arrested and Simon Peter was questioned, Peter denied he even knew him! Jesus had also warned him about his upcoming denial, and he still did it! And yet, he was the one who later led over 3,000 people toward faith in the person he had previously denied knowing.[54]

> "A wise person learns from their mistakes. A genius learns from somebody else's!"

I could go on and on with other examples, but you get the point. Every person who has achieved success has had to walk through failure, and you and I are no different. We all have to pass through that dark time of failure to get to the bright light of success. One word of warning: Mistakes happen. Failures happen. When you mess something up, you can come back. When you continually choose the same path upon which the failure occurred, it is no longer a mistake; it is a deliberate choice. You have the ability to *not* choose the wrong path. You have the ability to learn from your mistakes and become better. You can come back from failure!

Arguably one of the best basketball players in history, Michael Jordan was actually cut from his high school basketball team. But, to this day, nobody has touched his six NBA championships and five MVP awards. He said, "The key to success is failure."[55]

He also said this about failure in a famous Nike commercial: "I've missed more than 9,000 shots in my career. I've lost almost 300 games. Twenty-six times, I've been trusted to take the game-winning shot and missed. I've failed over and over and over again in my life. And that is why I succeed."

Michael Jordan has not only achieved incredible success as a basketball player, but also as an entrepreneur. He understands that only through the doorway of failure and evaluated experience is success found.

I love underdog movies, and the Rocky series has been a favorite of mine for my entire life. In the film *Rocky Balboa* (2006), Rocky looks at his son and makes this statement: "Life ain't about how hard you hit. It's about how hard you can get hit and keep moving forward."

Failure is only final if you give up and quit. As long as you are learning and moving forward, you're not done. In fact, you're on the verge of some of the greatest achievements of your life! Go for it! Remember, "It's not whether you get knocked down. It's whether you get back up." (Vince Lombardi.)[56]

> "The key to success is failure."

# CHAPTER 16

# TREAT EVERYONE THE SAME

## LEADERSHIP ILLUSION # 14

**T**he Effect: Treat every person you meet and work with exactly the same. That's only fair and equitable.

**The Secret:** Treating everyone the same exact way is not only wrong and unfair; it's also lazy. Everyone is different. They all process differently. They all have different temperaments. We have to learn their languages and speak their languages to them.

I was in Nicaragua with a pastor friend. We were in a convenience store, buying some drinks, and the owners realized my friend was the pastor in charge of a large group in their store. Because of their culture of honor, they immediately invited him to go behind the store to their house. There, they sat him in a large recliner and put a fan on him.

He sat there, lounging with his Coca-Cola in hand, and looked at the lady of the house. He said, "Your house is beautiful." The woman had a somewhat confused look on her face and shrugged her shoulders because she only spoke Spanish and didn't have a clue what he had just said to her.

My friend then looked at her and said slowly and more loudly, "You ... house ... beautiful." I snickered and whispered to him, "Say it slower and louder. She's gonna get it the next time." The woman, of course, still had a confused look on her face until I looked at her and said, *"Tu casa es muy bonita,"* to which she smiled broadly and said, *"Gracias!"*

It didn't matter how slowly or how loudly my friend spoke English to this woman; she only spoke Spanish, and she wasn't going to understand anything else. Why is this relevant? Because, although you may be speaking the same verbal language as someone, you may not be speaking the same *temperament* language.

I have four children. They're all very different. Sometimes, it's difficult to believe that they all came from the same parents, but they did. As a father, I started out trying to treat them the same, but they were all so different that they didn't respond to discipline in the same manner. My second daughter is a social butterfly. If I wanted to punish her, I took away her phone privileges. She would come back to me and beg me just to spank her and get the punishment over with! She couldn't stand not being able to talk to her friends on the phone. If I tried that same discipline on my oldest daughter, she would have been delighted. She would have gone to her room, read a book, and been perfectly content. I could not discipline my children in the same exact way because they are all very different. If you're a parent, you know exactly what I'm talking about.

All of us have different temperaments that are hard-wired into us from the moment we are born. When I realized how unfair it was to treat my kids as if they were the exact same person, I quickly understood that it was also a terrible practice when communicating with the people I worked with. After all, they are different people too!

When I was in high school, I knew a pair of identical twins named Rod and Rob. They looked exactly the same. Unless you knew them, it was almost impossible to tell them apart. But, when you looked at their actions, it was easy to know who was who. Rob was very quiet, studious, shy, and a neat freak. Rod was loud, funny, the life of every party, and a happy B/C student. You could laugh and joke with Rod. If you tried that with Rob, he would just stare at you. He was much more interested in talking about psychology and mathematics. They were identical twins in looks, but their personalities told very different stories. People can look the same but be very different in their temperaments.

> All of us have different temperaments that are hard-wired into us from the moment we are born.

I began studying the different personality styles and the DISC model of human behavior several years ago. Today, I am a certified human behavioral specialist in DISC. Since my certification, I've been privileged to go into all types of organizations and help them understand themselves and each other better and, ultimately, communicate more effectively and increase productivity.

The founder of Personality Insights[57] (the organization where I acquired my certification), Dr. Robert Rohm, made a statement that changed the way I looked at people forever. I hope it has the same effect on you. Dr. Rohm said, "We judge others by their actions, but we judge ourselves by our intent."[58] What does that mean? It means we take others at the face value of their actions but, when we do the same thing, we give ourselves the benefit of what we meant.

For example, when somebody shows up late, our normal first response is to say, "They're always late. That's so disrespectful!" But when *we're* late, we say, "Oh, the reason for that was _____," and, "I'm not normally this way, but _____ happened." Or, "Oh, I know that is what I said that but, what I *meant* was _____."

We give ourselves the benefit of the doubt. We judge ourselves by our intent or what we truly meant, regardless of what we actually did. But we don't give others that same benefit.

When I understood this statement and how each personality temperament wants different things, it opened up a whole new world of communication for me and allowed me to more deeply understand my team members. This was the key that unlocked the door to understanding myself and others.

> "We judge others by their actions, but we judge ourselves by our intent."

Don't worry. I'm not going to go into a long, boring, in-depth discussion of DISC. I *am* going to give you a brief overview of the four personality styles, but please remember that every single one of us is a unique blend of all four styles! If you're a leader, you'll need to understand that every one of these personality styles (or temperaments) is in your organization, and every one of them speaks a different temperament language. If you want to lead them, you'll need to become multilingual!

I'm going to list the four styles, along with a brief description of each. Everybody has one primary trait. It's their main style. Almost everyone has a secondary trait, and some even have a third one. For the purposes of this explanation, I'm just going to list the temperaments and their basic wants and needs:

- **D is the driven personality.** Their biggest desire is to win. They have an agenda that they're driving toward, and they don't like distractions that get in the way of that agenda.

They are the ones who get things done. Their intent is to get results. If they aren't producing, they aren't happy!

- **I is the inspiring personality.** Their biggest desire is to be liked. Their agenda is to be popular. They are the party people. Their intent is to have fun! If it isn't fun, they see no point in doing it!

- **S is the supportive personality.** Their biggest desire is to help others. Their agenda is to get along with others. Their intent is to help and support everyone. If there is conflict or loud talking, they are not at ease and will withdraw like a frightened turtle.

- **C is the cautious personality.** Their biggest desire is to do things right. Their agenda is for everything to be efficient and organized. Their intent is to be correct. If things are disorganized or inefficient, they will not only *not* be happy but they might also go on a crusade to straighten everyone out.

Once I understood the intent of the different personalities, I realized that nobody was trying to undermine me or hurt me. They were simply doing what they were made to do! They were operating the way they were designed to by their Creator. Each personality speaks the language of their intent, and it was my job to become multilingual so I could have a happy and productive team.

The D language was the easiest for me to speak because I am a D. For those who aren't, let me interpret their language. D-type personalities are bottom-line people. Don't say it in twenty words if you could say it in five. Their motto would be "Be brilliant, be brief, and be gone." They have a ton of things on their plate (by their own doing) and a ton to accomplish. Just give them the highlights of what you need.

I can already hear some of you screaming, "But wait! If I don't tell you every detail, how can you make an informed, correct decision?!" Let me help you here: A D-type personality doesn't need every detail, nor do they want it. They want the absolute bottom-line most important points, and they will make their decisions based on those. If you labor on too long with details, their built-in ADD (attention deficit disorder) will kick in, and they will check out of the conversation. If they want to or need to know more, they'll ask questions. If you're talking to a D, be *direct* and to the point. They'll appreciate it. This is their language!

The I language is my secondary trait. I am very close to this one too. Their language is fun! Be sure and smile a lot when you talk to them. Remember that they want to be liked! Your smile can be the difference between a fruitful conversation and a dramatic disaster. If you have a fun story you can lead with, do it. I-type personalities love entertaining stories! But be ready to patiently listen to the story they will subsequently tell you that will probably one-up the one you just told them. Be sure and laugh and tell them how much you enjoyed it. Also, if there is something else they have done well, be sure to commend them on it. I-types love positive recognition, especially in front of their peers. I-types also are not detail people. When communicating with them, you want to emphasize how much fun the situation can be and/or how it can make them look good and be more popular. If you're talking to an I, be *interesting, inspiring, fun,* and *smile!* This is their language!

The S language is foreign to me. It's my lowest score. I had to learn this language, and it was a labor. Interestingly enough, it also represents the largest percentage of the population so, if you don't know this language, you should definitely learn it. S-type personalities are far and away the sweetest people you will meet. The worst thing you can say to an S is anything in a loud or raised voice. Be conscious of your vocal tones and lower your voice, especially if you're a D or an I! Your natural tones of being direct and excited will be intimidating to them. Speak softly and sincerely. Look them in the eyes. Let them know they are appreciated. Remember that they love to know that what they are doing matters and is appreciated. Instead of expressing that in front of people (that's a big no-no for this temperament), consider writing a handwritten note. They will appreciate it. If you're talking to an S, be *sincere* and *sweet* and choose your words carefully. They are the most sensitive of all of the personalities. This is their language!

The C language is the language of details and efficiency. If you're talking to a C, you'd better have your ducks in a row and know what you're talking about. Nothing will elicit a negative response from a C any quicker than being wrong in your information or falsely accusing them of being wrong. Personality types who don't usually give details must learn to provide lots of details when talking to a C. C-type personalities will be convinced to join your team only if they've been given enough correct information to make an informed decision. You'll have to go over all that information with them and then expect them to ask you for a day or so to think about it while they go research what you've told them to make sure it's correct. I used to think this meant they didn't trust me. That's not true. They simply despise being incorrect and want to research everything to make sure they aren't. If they do something based on what someone has told them and it turns out to be incorrect information, they will blame themselves much more for not researching it better than they will blame the person who told them. If you're talking to a C, be *detailed* and *correct* in your information. This is their language!

Years ago, my father took me to a theme park in Nashville called Opryland USA. There was a roller coaster there called the Wabash Cannonball. It had a large drop and two corkscrew loops. I was ten years old. My father was one of the best "people readers" I have ever known. He didn't study DISC, but he was a master of knowing and understanding people. As we approached this monster, my father looked at the fear in my face and, knowing my D personality style, asked me, "Are you ready to ride this?" I timidly replied, "I don't know." He then asked a key question for my temperament: "You're not going to let this conquer you, are you?" I resolutely replied, "*No*," and off we went into the line.

When I boarded the roller coaster, I started crying. As we went up the hill, the tears continued to flow. My father put his hand on my leg and told me it would be okay. We took off at the top of the hill and, as the coaster dropped down the hill and went through the inversions, I cried more. When we pulled into the station, my father looked at me and asked, "So? What'd you think?" Through tears and sniffling, I looked back at him and said, "Can we do it again?" And of course, we did.

I have four kids. They are all very different. I'll just list their strongest temperaments, but remember that every person is a unique blend of all the temperaments. My oldest daughter is a C-type personality. My second daughter is an I-type. Both of my sons have primarily S-type personality styles.

Many years ago, I was at Six Flags in Georgia with my oldest daughter, who was ten years old at the time. As we approached the wooden roller coaster, the Georgia Cyclone, I could see the fear in her eyes. I asked her, "Are you ready to ride this?" She timidly replied, "I don't know." I asked her, "Are you going to let this conquer you?" She looked up at the roller coaster and replied in a trembling voice, "Yeah ..." I talked her into coming with me anyway.

We got in line and she kept asking me questions. "How high is this rollercoaster? How fast does it go? It is really scary?"

Do you see it? She was screaming in her language, but I wasn't hearing her! She was telling me she wasn't primarily a driven personality. She was a cautious personality!

Being deaf to her temperament language, I just kept reassuring her. At one point she wanted to leave the line and I told her again that it would be fine. She finally agreed to go through with it and said, "Okay. I'll ride it … but not on the front row!" I said, "That's fine. We'll ride in the back." She agreed. I, of course, knew that the back was the much wilder ride and thought it would be good for her.

We boarded the coaster and she hung onto my arm for dear life. As we went flying down the first monstrous drop, she screamed and began to cry. As we topped the hills, we were getting major air time. She cried all the way through the ride. At the end of the ride, we pulled into the station, and I looked at her just like my father had looked at me and asked, "So? What'd you think?"

She looked at me shouted, *"What kind of father are you?! This is the worst ride ever! I'll never believe anything you say ever again!"* and then she stormed off the coaster.

I was shocked! It didn't work at all as it had with my father. I ended up chasing her down and apologizing profusely. The good news is that, today, she will ride any roller coaster with me.

However, I learned a valuable lesson that day. I made the assumption that she processed things like I did. I assumed we spoke the same language. This is the same problem happening with leaders all over the world. We think we're communicating clearly when we're actually not even speaking their language. My daughter and I had very different personality styles, and what motivated me frightened her to death. I had to adjust my style to hers. I had to learn to speak her language, which I eventually did.

My second daughter wore platform-heel shoes to a theme park all day just to be tall enough to ride a rollercoaster—not only because she wanted to ride it but because, if she wasn't tall enough, she was afraid she would miss out on some fun that other people were having. That is such an I-type thing to do!

My two daughters are very different. So are the people working on your team. They all have different wants, desires, and fears. They all speak different temperament languages. And they all look to you as their leader to be able to speak those languages.

There's only so much we can cover about DISC and personality languages in one chapter, but the suggestions in this chapter can start you on the road to an understanding and communication that your team members will notice and appreciate.

Suffice to say, recognizing the importance of flexibility in communication is critical for a leader to understand. Only through such understanding can they learn to move fluently through the style of each language in order to relate to people and lead them effectively. Treating everyone the exact same way is one of the most selfish and unfair things we can do as leaders. A true leader will value the diversity of styles in their team and treat people according to *their* needs, not the leader's needs.

> We think we're communicating clearly when we're actually not even speaking their language.

# CHAPTER 17

# CRITICISM IS YOUR ENEMY

**T**he Effect: Criticism from people has to be completely eliminated from your life. If someone criticizes you, shut them out. If someone who works with you or for you is critical of you, get rid of them from your life.

**The Secret:** Criticism is an excellent opportunity for personal growth if it's put in its proper perspective. Weak and ineffective leaders surround themselves with people who always agree with them. It is one of the biggest mistakes a leader can make. When criticism becomes personal, you have to guard yourself, but always look for the thread of truth in it, because that is a key to personal growth.

The first pastor I ever really got to know was a man named Fred Ward. He was an incredible leader for many reasons. He had worked in the industry for almost twenty years. He was a results-oriented person. With him, it was all about the bottom line. Having the same D-type temperament (see the previous chapter), we hit it off and got along well.

As a driven young man, I knew how to get results. I could inspire and motivate people. I was good at recruiting and growing. There was just one problem: I would make boneheaded mistakes. I would say things that would upset people. I was so focused on the task that I often hurt people in the process of accomplishing a goal.

Fred would sit me down and talk to me. I have to admit that, at first, I thought he was schizophrenic. He would get red-faced and berate my actions and tell me how dumb it was to do what I had done. I would practically be in tears and ready to slit my wrists from the way he talked to me—and then, at the end, he'd smile and say, "Okay, let's go get something to eat."

I'd think, *What?!*

I finally talked to him about it and asked how he could be so mad and upset at me and still want to go somewhere with me right afterward. He imparted an important lesson he had learned in the industry. He simply told me, "I'm not mad at you. I was mad at what you did. You're better than that. You knew better than that. If I didn't believe you were capable of more, I wouldn't have said so much, but I know you're more than the way you're acting. I attacked your actions. I did not attack you. I love you. I just don't like what you did."

Once I understood that Fred loved me, he earned the right to tell me anything he needed to say to me. I realized that when he was critical of my mistakes, it was only because he wanted me to be better as a leader. His mentoring and constructive criticism changed my life, but only because I recognized and received it and applied the lessons.

During my time at the church, I also witnessed church members attacking the decisions Fred made. Some people were just naturally critical. When I asked Fred about how he handled it, he would say, "It's not personal. It's just business." And most of the time, he was exactly right. They weren't attacking him personally; they just didn't like what he was doing. When I began to see the difference in those two things, it helped me put criticism in its proper perspective. You have to separate the problem from the person, and this skill is often missed by many people.

> ## "It's not personal.
> ## It's just business."

There are two types of criticism. There is criticism concerning what someone said or did, and there is criticism of who someone is or what they are attempting to do. We'll deal with the first one (what someone said or did) here:

1) Learn the difference between personal attacks and legitimate criticism. "You shouldn't have done that" is talking about the problem and what you did. "You are a bad person" is a personal attack. When you remove emotion from the equation, which is a necessary element, ask yourself if they are really attacking you as a person or if they are criticizing what you said or did (which is not necessarily who you are).

2) When do you evaluate the criticism, is there any truth in it? Imagine somebody else had said or done what you did. Would the criticism that was leveled at your actions be valid if it was toward them?

3) Write out any truth in the criticism and use it as an opportunity to improve as a person and a leader. Think of this as a *Reader's Digest*. For those who don't know, *Reader's Digest* was a small monthly magazine filled with articles, quotes, and other interesting items. I personally never knew of anyone who read it from cover to cover each month; you would just pick and choose what applied to you and ignore the rest. I think that's a great way to treat criticism: Pick and choose what is applicable and ignore the rest—it's irrelevant.

4) Look at your team and see if they're all "yes" people. Weak leaders surround themselves only with those who tell them they're great. Effective leaders know there is something

wonderful about healthy debate and disagreements that cause massive growth in individuals and organizations. If two people always think the same thing, one of them is unnecessary. Does your team genuinely reflect a diversity of thought and ideas? "Look for people whose skills are the opposite of yours. Dare to emphasize your weaknesses." (Diane Janknegt.)[59]

5) As a leader, if you have to be critical of someone's actions or words, always do it privately and be conscious of attacking the problem while affirming the person. Remember what we said earlier about boiling water? Start by affirming the person. Let them know you value them personally before dealing with what they did. Attack the actions, not the person! Always end by affirming them, as well.

Now let's deal with the second type of criticism. Sometimes, people are critical of others simply to derail them or hurt them. They make it a personal attack. How do you handle that?

1) Consider the source. Is the person who was critical of you someone you would emulate? Do they have the life that you would like to have? Do they exemplify the type of person you want to become in life? If the answer to all of those questions is "no," then ask yourself why you care what they think.

2) I heard Darren Hardy say it this way: "Only about ten people will cry at your funeral. And out of that ten, the deciding factor on whether most of them will attend your graveside service will be whether or not it is raining outside. When someone is critical of me, I ask myself, 'Will they be crying at my funeral?' If the answer is 'no,' then why do I care what they think?!" I think that's a great way to look at it.

3) If someone personally attacks you or your family, keep your boundaries well-defined and secure. Attacking someone personally is never right, no matter the situation. If someone

makes it personal, politely but firmly remind them that they are welcome to criticize your work, but you and your family are off-limit subjects.

4) Does the person who criticized what you were attempting to do genuinely care about you? This is a tough one to know because, sometimes, criticism is leveled at us by those we are closest to (like family, for instance). I know of many examples where a person was attempting to gain financial freedom or pursue a lifelong dream in a career or some other lofty goal, and their close family members were some of the ones telling them, "It'll never work!" or, "Who do you think you are?" or, "You'll only get hurt if you try!" or (my favorite), "I tried it before, and it didn't work!"

Remember the principle of the crab. I used to live in Florida on the Gulf Coast. If you were to go to the best seafood places on the coast, they were the ones in ramshackle huts that looked like a strong wind would blow them over. If they served crabs, you would often see large buckets in front of the restaurant with crabs in them. The buckets never had lids. Do you know why? If one crab was placed in the bucket, it would simply crawl out. But if two or more crabs were in a bucket and one tried to crawl out, the other crab(s) would grab the one trying to escape and pull him back down into the bucket. If the crab persisted in trying to get out, the other crabs would tear off its claws and eventually kill it. Crabs that stayed in the bottom of the bucket were never bothered. They all just sat there, waiting to be cooked and eaten.

When you attempt to pursue your dream and destiny, expect the "crabs" to show up and try to pull you back into reality—in particular, *their* reality. The truth is, they don't want you to succeed because, if you actually accomplish what you are setting out to do, it will make them feel bad about not succeeding themselves. They'll dispute that but, in the end, it is true. They would rather everyone stay at the bottom of the bucket of mediocrity and exist with them in misery, awaiting the same fate as everyone else.

But you are meant for more! You need to eliminate the crabs from your life. I'm not suggesting cutting yourself off from your family or close friends, but I am recommending you minimize their negative input in your life. Jim Rohn said that if you take the five people you hang around the most and average out their salaries, that's what you'll be making in about five years.[60] That statement either really scares you or it affirms who you're hanging around with. I'm not suggesting that money is the path to happiness or success but, as Zig Ziglar once said, "Money isn't everything, but it ranks right up there with oxygen."[61] If you want to have success and live your dreams, you need to ignore those who criticize your dreams and then go on pursuing them. Realize you're going to have people—even well-meaning ones—who will attempt to derail you from your purpose in life. Sometimes, their intent is to keep you from getting hurt, but we both know you're stronger than that. You know you're going to get hurt and fail, but you're going to get back up and press on to your dream!

> Ignore those who criticize your dreams and then go on pursuing them.

1) Overcome that horrible two-letter word "no." It seems in life that people would rather do anything than hear the word "no." They do everything they can to avoid it. But that's the opposite of what you need to do. Embrace it! In fact, go after it. Keep in mind that every "no" you receive moves you

closer to your "yes." And one "yes" can change your life! If you're growing and learning and improving and working on your personal growth, then the "yes" will eventually happen—if you don't give up. Some of the biggest successes we know today went through their "no" too:

a) Joanne was told her book wasn't good, and it was rejected by publishers twelve different times. But Joanne K. Rowling persisted, and nearly everyone in the world today knows who Harry Potter is.[62]

b) Fred wrote a paper in college about an overnight delivery service and received a "C" because his Yale professor said the idea wasn't feasible. But Fred Smith went on to found Federal Express and made the unfeasible idea a reality that changed the world. For years in their advertisements, when a package was pictured, the return address in the photo was the address of Yale University.[63]

c) Walt had an idea for a movie that was a "space opera." Every studio he took it to said it was not only too "out there," but it was impossible to actually make. Finally, one struggling studio took on the idea. The struggling studio was 20th Century Fox. Walt's full name is George Walton Lucas, and his movie was called *Star Wars*. It became the highest grossing movie of its time. As to the impossibility of making the movie, Lucas founded Lucasfilm Ltd. and Skywalker Sound, which not only made the impossible a reality but also revolutionized how movies are made to this day. It's hard to find a movie today that doesn't have those two company names in its credits.[64]

d) Jack had an idea for a book that was rejected 144 times. That's twelve times per month for a year. Most people give up after one or two rejections. He experienced *144* of them. But, finally, a publisher picked up his book, and we all know the success Jack Canfield had selling millions and millions of copies of *Chicken Soup for the Soul*.[65]

If you are willing to press through the "no" of the critics and "experts" who say your dream is impossible then you will make it to the other side and see your vision become a reality.

Just as anyone who has achieved success has gone through the pathway of failure, they've also gone through the barbs of criticism. Twentieth-century philosopher Elbert Hubbard said, "If you want to escape moral and physical assassination, do nothing, say nothing, and be nothing—court obscurity, for only in oblivion does safety lie."[66] I believe that's right. But I think the best quote on critics and criticism I've ever heard comes from our twenty-sixth president of the United States, Theodore Roosevelt:

> *It is not the critic who counts; not the man who points out how the strong man stumbles, or where the doer of deeds could have done them better. The credit belongs to the man who is actually in the arena, whose face is marred by dust and sweat and blood; who strives valiantly; who errs, who comes short again and again, because there is no effort without error and shortcoming; but who does actually strive to do the deeds; who knows great enthusiasms, the great devotions; who spends himself in a worthy cause; who at the best knows in the end the triumph of high achievement, and who at the worst, if he fails, at least fails while daring greatly, so that his place shall never be with those cold and timid souls who neither know victory nor defeat.*[67]

Don't let critics sideline you. If there is something valid in the criticism, then take it, learn from it, and throw away the rest. Keep pressing forward, leader! Only you can accomplish the vision that is inside of you!

If you're leading a team, look for those people who aren't like you and don't think like you. There is great value in a diversity of opinions. If two people on a team are exactly alike, one of them isn't necessary.

Criticism can be your best friend and your worst enemy at the same time. It's all in how you process it.

And remember what Fred taught me: "It's not personal."

Just as anyone who has achieved
success has gone through the
pathway of failure,
they've also gone through the
barbs of criticism.

# CHAPTER 18

# CONFIDENCE IS
# THE OPPOSITE OF HUMILITY

---

LEADERSHIP ILLUSION # 16

---

**T**he **Effect**: You cannot be confident and be a humble person at the same time.

**The Secret**: Confidence is not the opposite of humility. Arrogance is the opposite of humility. Arrogance is often misplaced confidence. True confidence is knowing the abilities you have are a gift to be used in the service of others. That is the highest form of service and humility a person can have.

Douglas MacArthur was arguably one of the greatest military leaders in American history. He became the youngest army general at the age of fifty and was the best-known of all of them. He was a charismatic figure known for his bravado. His military maneuvers, especially during World War II, brought inspiration to millions of Americans, who considered him a hero. He stood up to the Japanese empire that had bombed Pearl Harbor. When he was forced out of the Philippines back into Australia by the Japanese, he famously declared, "I shall return!" He was known for making speeches and for his strong opinions. He was also known for occasionally ignoring the orders of his superiors if he felt his way was better.

Harry Truman had very humble beginnings. He was a shy and sickly child. He wasn't an athlete. His parents were not wealthy. He wasn't a particularly stellar student, but he was a voracious reader. He never graduated from college (the only US president of the twentieth century who didn't). He served honorably in World War I and became the commander of his battery. He experienced failure in a haberdashery business in his hometown of Independence, Missouri, but found modest success as a politician serving as a county judge. In 1934, he was elected to the United States Senate.

He gained some prominence as a senator for his "Truman Committee," which focused on eliminating wasteful government spending. In 1944, he was reluctantly chosen by Franklin Roosevelt as the vice presidential candidate to bring a more centrist view to their ticket. When Roosevelt died in 1945, Harry Truman became the thirty-third president of the United States.

From the beginning, his presidency was fraught with controversy. He used the atomic bomb twice on Japan to end World War II. He was considered to be an unrefined, uneducated, ignorant man who had accidentally ascended to the presidency. His approval ratings were abysmal.

So it should come as no surprise that when, in 1950, President Truman had a conflict with General MacArthur, the general population favored MacArthur. After all, he was a war hero. Harry Truman had surprised everyone in 1948 when he was actually elected to the presidency, defeating his popular opponent from New York, Thomas Dewey.

Although he was accused by his critics of being uneducated and arrogant, Harry Truman was an exceptionally humble man. He would spread around the credit for his administration's accomplishments to others. He continuously empowered others to succeed. He also took the blame for the things that went wrong. In fact, Truman had a desk sign that read, "The buck stops here," which meant when others "passed the buck" and played the blame game, Truman took ultimate responsibility for what happened. He had confidence in his knowledge of history, his experience in politics, the advice of his close counselors, and his authority as the president of the United States.

Douglas MacArthur was arrogant. He didn't listen to others, nor did he feel he needed advice from others. He thought he knew what was best for our military and our world, and he had no trouble telling everyone why he was right. And here's the thing: On many of his points, he probably *was* right. It could even be argued that there wouldn't be a North and South Korea today if MacArthur had been allowed to finish his military campaign. MacArthur also wanted to bomb communist China and take it over. He was beyond ambitious.

President Truman was erring on the side of discretion, however, and opted for a peaceful approach to the Korean War. MacArthur disagreed and pushed for a full military solution. In other words, he wanted to conquer Korea. As we've said previously, disagreement between leaders can be healthy. It can produce better results but, in this case, MacArthur chose to take his case to the news outlets and tell them why he thought Truman was wrong. In his mind, Truman was a country hick who didn't know what MacArthur knew about war. He publicly voiced his disagreement with Truman and his decisions.

The end reult? President Harry Truman fired General Douglas MacArthur in April 1951. It was considered one of the most unpopular decisions Truman ever made. Later on, when he was asked about that decision, Truman replied, "I fired him because he disrespected the office of the president and you don't do that." History has now proven him right. Why? Because Truman knew that if he allowed a military commander to usurp the president's authority then another military commander could take more authority and exercise a military coup against the United States. There is little doubt among historians today that if General MacArthur had continued unchecked, it would have led America into a sustained war in Asia (and, if you know the history of land wars in Asia, those are never good!).

MacArthur forgot an essential rule of leadership: Before you can be in authority, you must learn to operate *under* authority. Even though his points may have been valid, the manner in which he shared them publicly caused a crisis of authority and leadership. Douglas MacArthur was sure he was right and that his way was the only way. He was exceedingly arrogant and wasn't listening to anyone else. Harry Truman wasn't arrogant. He just had supreme confidence in his authority as president. He had been a lifelong student of history and had studied biographies of leaders as well as war strategies. He knew it wasn't in the best interest of the American people, freedom, or peace in the world to allow MacArthur to continue his course of action.

> Before you can be in authority, you must learn to operate under authority.

Many times, people confuse arrogance with confidence. Here's the principle difference: Arrogance serves your own purposes and agenda, while confidence knows what your gifts and abilities are and that they're made to serve the best interests of others.

So the question is, what gifts or abilities do you possess? This may seem like an easy question, but it really isn't. Many people have trouble honestly discussing their own strengths. Our natural inclination is to be open about our faults and shortcomings. We are often our own worst critics. Take a moment and list your strengths, gifts, talents, and abilities. Take your time. Don't move on to the next paragraph until you've completed this.

Next, it is essential to realize that our gifts and abilities are not ours. We're merely renting them. Your gifts don't go with you when you die. Neither does anything else. In fact, everything we think we have or own, we don't. The moment we die, it becomes somebody else's. I have had the unfortunate circumstance of witnessing siblings fighting over money and property after a parent's death (the parent having not prepared a will). It divides families, sometimes for a lifetime. I've always thought about how grieved the parents would have been had they known how the children would fight over things—things that are just as temporary as life itself.

> Arrogance serves your own purposes and agenda, while confidence knows what your gifts and abilities are and that they're made to serve the best interests of others.

So if we understand that everything we own or think we have is not really ours, then we can focus on something much higher: How is what we've been given going to be best used?

That brings us to the next question, and the next question is crucial: How are you using the things you've just listed to benefit others? This is the key between confidence and arrogance. Arrogance only cares about what it knows and how it can benefit itself. Confidence knows that every ability is a gift to help someone else.

A gift is not truly a gift until it is given away and accepted by someone else. A Christmas present that stays wrapped in your house all year that you forget to give someone isn't truly a gift; it's just a box in your house. (Not at all saying I've done this … okay, I have. I found it in my closet in May and had to give it as a "birthday" present a week late to someone.)

Everything we've been given is meant to be a gift we use to help someone else. But here's the catch: When we help others, we always end up helping ourselves. I cannot explain this but, somehow, when we give, we almost inevitably end up getting back far more than we gave. Remember, "No one has ever become poor by giving." (Anne Frank.)[68] Some of the most generous people I've ever met are also usually the wealthiest. But they aren't generous because they're wealthy. The truth is, they're wealthy because they're generous.

Last of all, look at your list. Everything on that list is God's gift to you to be used to bless others. When someone is good at something but still says, "I'm not all that good at that," that is not humility. That's actually false humility.

When someone says, "God has gifted me in this area, and I know the abilities I've been given can serve this organization," or, "I believe that my gifts can help you," that is confidence. It is not arrogance.

> "No one has ever become poor by giving."

If I am about to have surgery on my heart, I do not want a cardiologist looking at me and saying, "Yeah, I'm not all that good."

I want him to have confidence. I want him to say, "I've studied, and I've done thousands of these procedures. I know the gifts I've been given to help others, and you're going to be just fine." The first statement is false humility, and it doesn't inspire anyone to follow you. The second statement is true confidence that people will follow.

Arrogance is most often a false belief in what you can do, and it is always self-seeking and self-centered. It seeks attention and recognition. It will run over others to get it too. Arrogance seeks out powerful people to acquire more power for itself. Given the opportunity, it will take credit for not only what *it* does, but what *others* do as well. If a doctor says, "Yeah! I'm the best doctor in the entire world! I got this! I've done this surgery a million times!" that type of exaggeration and arrogance will not inspire confidence in anyone.

Arrogance centers around individuals and attempting to make others think more of that person than they should.

Confidence is a belief in what a person can do to help others. That person believes in their ability but will also spread the credit around where it is due. It empowers others to grow and succeed. It works hand in hand with true humility.

Here's what arrogance and confidence look like side by side:

| Arrogance | Confidence |
|---|---|
| No substance to back up beliefs. | Has substance to back up beliefs. |
| Seeks more power for itself. | Seeks to empower others. |
| Takes credit for everything. | Spreads credit around to the team. |
| Believes it's the best. | Knows there are others who are better. |
| Talks about itself constantly. | Gets others to talk about themselves. |

| Wants to be liked by others at all costs. | Knows it is more important to connect with others. |
| Thrives on public recognition. | Thrives on giving away recognition. |
| Wants to promote self above all to gain position or title. | Wants to empower and promote others to step into their destiny. |

As leaders, we have to be confident in our abilities to help others. Helping and serving others is the highest calling a leader can have. Remember, "No one is useless in this world who lightens the burdens of another." (Charles Dickens.)[69] And also, "No definition of a successful life can do anything but include serving others." (George H. W. Bush.)[70]

Bill Gates and Steve Jobs are known for advancing the human race in terms of computer technology. They originally started out working together but ended up parting ways.

Bill was a more humble, quiet person. He was extremely proficient in business ideas and knew how to assemble effective teams around him to accomplish his plans. He was known for being highly approachable and down to earth in his communication. Bill, as most of you know, founded Microsoft.

Steve was known for being louder and arrogant. He was difficult to say anything to because he felt he mostly knew it all. His brash approach turned lots of people off, including Bill Gates, but he did get the job done. Despite being challenging to work with, he accomplished a great deal and brought the world the iPhone, the iPad, and iTunes. Steve founded Apple.

The conflict between Microsoft and Apple is legendary. Steve Jobs accused Bill Gates of stealing his platform and ideas when Windows was released. Bill Gates accused Steve Jobs of being out of touch with reality, saying the concept for both platforms came from Xerox. Jobs said Gates was a stick in the mud with no mind for business. Gates said Jobs had a knack for design and sales but had no mind for technology. I could go on and on …

Today, Microsoft and Apple users are as loyal to their brands and as far apart philosophically as Democrats and Republicans in America, despite the similarities in both products! I know there are people probably screaming at the last sentence on that page for multiple reasons. The truth is, *both* men were brilliant, *both* had terrific ideas, and *both* accomplished amazing things.

Steve Jobs focused on the look and the marketing, which, even after his death, Apple is still known for. Apple users favor sleek designs and are among the most loyal users in the world today. (For the record, I'm typing this book on a Mac.) They have an incredible marketing team that relates to their customers directly and uniquely. Jobs was focused much more on the company than he was on the people and his team.

Bill Gates was focused on the power of the computer and on bringing it into the hands of every person on the planet. Thirty years ago, a computer was a luxury in a home. Today, it is a necessity, and hardly anyone can imagine life without one. Bill Gates made that dream a reality. His focus was on the people and his team much more than the company.

Steve Jobs built the largest company in the world. Bill Gates was the richest man in the world and could have remained the richest man if he hadn't changed his focus from running Microsoft to philanthropy (giving his money away).

I'm not saying one man is better than the other, but it is pretty clear that one man made it all about other people, while the other was more focused on how the company and how things looked.

True leaders are humble but confident individuals. They acknowledge that their successes come from team efforts and spread the accolades around. They know what they're good at but they don't flaunt those abilities. They simply use them to better their organization and other individuals. They use their gifts to propel others forward. They know that when they bless others, their own lives will be blessed as well.

As Zig Ziglar famously said, "You can get everything in life you want if you help enough people get what they want."[71] Having confidence in your abilities (that you use to help others get what they want or need) is one of the highest forms of leadership anywhere. It's about serving *their* needs. Remember, "The greatest among you must be the servant of all." (Matthew 23:11.)

"You can get everything in life you want if you help enough people get what they want."

# CHAPTER 19

# ASSUME EVERYONE KNOWS

**T**he Effect: "I said it, so they heard it."

**The Secret:** Saying something doesn't mean that person heard anything. Communication is a multifaceted flow of information that goes both ways. Left unchecked, it has derailed many a leader and many an organization.

Elaine was one of the nicest and most giving women I knew. She was always immaculately dressed and, although she was a true professional woman in a thriving business, she was always willing to volunteer and help other people, especially in their times of need. She had been through a bad marriage and had rebuilt her life as a successful single woman. There was a lot to admire about her.

So when she came to me and told me she had met a wonderful man whom she wanted to marry and asked me if I would perform their wedding ceremony, I was honored to say yes. Michael was a tremendous guy who loved Elaine. In fact, the look in his eyes when he saw her told me that he adored her. I did their premarital counseling at the church. It was the easiest counseling session I've ever done. They scored the highest of any couple on their compatibility evaluation, especially in the area of realistic expectations about relationships. If any couple was made for each other, it was Michael and Elaine.

We were two weeks away from the wedding, all counseling sessions had been completed, and I was eating with my family at a local restaurant. You can imagine my surprise when I looked from my booth to the bar area and saw Elaine sitting cuddled up next to a man who was not Michael.

I got a sick feeling in the middle of my stomach. I looked closer and reasoned on my insides, "Maybe that's her brother?"

Then she gave him a passionate kiss. It was definitely not her brother.

I knew I was going to have to confront her. I thought of poor Michael and how devastated he would be when he found out. I began to get angry and thought, *How could she do this to him? He's such a great guy! He loves her!*

I wasn't going to wait, so I got up from my booth and began to walk toward the bar area where they were seated. As I stood up, I saw Elaine stand up with the man, give him another kiss, and, with grasped hands, begin to walk toward the exit.

I steeled my courage—I knew this was going to be a very ugly confrontation. Elaine and the man were walking toward me, but they made absolutely no move to avoid me and showed no expressions of shock (unlike my own face!), even though I was pretty sure they had seen me.

I took a deep breath and, as I was almost face-to-face with them, the word "Elaine" poised on my lips, I felt a tap on my shoulder.

I turned around. It was Elaine.

She grinned broadly and hugged me and said, "Oh, Ken! Have you met my twin sister, Ellie?"

I looked at Elaine and looked back at Ellie. Then I looked again. I'm pretty sure it was a triple take. They were indeed identical twins.

I looked back at Elaine and replied, "No. I haven't met Ellie, but I've never been happier to meet anybody in my entire life!" A wave of relief washed over me and, after I explained my perspective, they all got a huge laugh out the situation. I'm happy to report that, over twelve years later, Elaine and Michael are still happily married and still adore each other.

Elaine was a twin. In all the time I'd known her and in all of those premarital counseling sessions, that little detail had never come up. That was information I could have used that night.

Sometimes, we think we're genuinely communicating or that we really have a handle on the situation, but many times we're wrong. One little detail can change the entire situation and, if we're not well-informed, we'll make incorrect assumptions and end up with our feet in our mouths (or down the throat, in my case)!

When we assume communication has happened, we often end up in bad situations and wonder how we got there. We may think we told somebody something, and perhaps we did, but telling someone something and them actually hearing what we said—and understanding it—are two remarkably different things.

I will confess: I was terrible at communication. I assumed that, just because I'd said something, others had understood it. When things didn't happen as I wanted, I would get upset and say, "I told you that!" I didn't truly communicate; I dumped. I had something on my checklist and, as soon as I told someone, I would cross it off my list. I wasn't communicating at all. I was simply telling and not taking the time to even know if the person understood what I was saying.

> One little detail can change the entire situation.

Communication—true communication—takes time. It takes time to get to know each other's unique communication styles (see chapter 16, "Treat Everyone the Same"), it takes time to understand how people process information, and, most of all, it takes hard work to be an excellent communicator.

Here are a few tips that helped me in this area. Ask yourself:

1) **Do you talk more than you listen?** Driven personalities (D-types) and inspiring personalities (I-types) like to talk. I'm a mix of both of those, so talking comes naturally for me. Unfortunately, listening does not. I heard someone say, "God gave you two ears and one mouth for a reason!" Many times, it would benefit us as leaders to keep silent and really listen to what our team is saying. My father used to say, "Better to be silent and thought a fool than to speak and erase all doubt." Listening is an art form that takes practice. All of us have the ability within us to be great listeners. If you take the percentage of time you spend talking versus the time you spend listening and find that talking far outweighs listening then you need to make an adjustment now. Here's what I did: Once I understood what my problem was, I purposed to make myself not talk—even if I knew the answer and even if I had a witty or funny reply. I purposed to keep my mouth shut. But that was only half of the battle. Next, I had to tune my ears to really hear what people were saying. This took some time and quite a bit of trial and error. I'll cover the method in number 3 below. Listening is the key that unlocks the door to communication. Most people think it's what we say, but what we hear is far more critical! Remember, "Courage is what it takes to stand up and speak; courage is also what it takes to sit down and listen."[72]

2) **Do you formulate your answer before the other person is even finished speaking?** Before we can talk about the method, we have to address this vital question. I used to do this all of the time. I would listen until I thought I had heard enough information to formulate a reply and then I'd check out of what that person was saying and wait for a break so I could jump in with my response. I enjoy watching the show *Family Feud* occasionally. Every now and then, you'll see someone in the first round hit the buzzer to answer a question

before the host is done reading the question. They assume they know the answer, and some of the answers they give after the full question has been read are nothing short of hilarious. You can look them up on YouTube. Well, I had a bad habit of doing the same thing. Sometimes, I'd cut a person off with my "all-important reply" and "wisdom and knowledge," and most people were kind and aware enough to just let me rattle on. I thought I was being smart. I was actually being an insensitive, rude jerk. Sometimes, it was even more embarrassing when my "wise reply" actually had nothing to do with what they were actually talking about. There is rarely, if ever, a good reason to cut somebody off, and all it does is tell the person speaking that you don't respect their viewpoints. Listening is always more important than talking. *Always*. As an old Turkish proverb says, "If speaking is silver, listening is gold." When someone else is speaking, look them in the eyes, listen to their words, and observe their tone and body language. All of those aspects contribute to effective listening. Dr. Albert Mehrabian, professor emeritus at UCLA and author of *Silent Messages*, concluded that a whopping 93 percent of all communication is nonverbal![73] That means 93 percent of what we're saying isn't even coming out of our mouths. It's our facial expressions, our body language, our demeanor, our attitude. These far outweigh our words. When we listen, we have to be aware of more than the words the person is saying. We must factor in all of the nonverbal cues as well.

3) **Have you ever used reflective listening?** Reflective listening is a technique used to establish effective communication. Although easy to do, it is difficult to perfect. Think about a mirror. A mirror merely reflects what it is in front of it. Reflective listening means you reflect back to the person what you believe they said. Here's an example:

   • Person A says, "I didn't like the way that report was worded."

- Person B reflects, "I heard you say you didn't like how I write."

- Person A then reiterates, "No. I said I didn't like the way this report was worded. I actually like the way you write."

- Person B then says, "I heard you say you didn't like this report."

- Person A then clarifies, "I like the report. There are just a couple of sentences that I think need revising, but overall I like the report."

- Person B then says, "I heard you say you want a couple of sentences in this report to be revised, but overall you like it."

- Person A then confirms, "Yes. That's exactly what I said."

> "God gave you two ears and one mouth for a reason!"

Do you see how each reflection brings the people closer to accurate and true communication? With reflective listening, each person reflects back what the other individual is saying until authentic communication is achieved. One of three things are going to happen when you reflect back to someone what you believe they just said:

a) They will realize you didn't hear what they said at all, and they'll either repeat it or revise how they said it to be more precise.

b) They will realize you reflected back exactly what they said, and it may be not what they meant to say. They'll then change their statement to be closer to what they actually intended.

c) They'll hear you say exactly what they said and will confirm to you that you have heard them.

> ## 93 percent of all communication is nonverbal!

Remember: True communication doesn't happen until you've spoken it and the person (or people) you're talking to responds in such a way that lets you know they have heard you and understand your meaning. Real communication is always in a connected, continuous loop between the person speaking and the person listening.

1) **Write down what you thought you heard them say.** If you write down what you thought you heard the person say, you have a reference to return to when your listening senses are more attuned. In writing down what I thought I heard and then revisiting it an hour or a day or two later, I was relieved that I didn't actually try to reflect what I had heard. I would have been way off base.

2) **Be willing to try and fail.** Writing it down for you to evaluate later is a safer way to learn your listening skills, but ultimately you have to be willing to try and fail. You're not going to get it right every time. Nobody does. But the good news is that the more you do it, the better you'll get at it and the quicker you'll be speaking other people's languages. When you get it wrong, apologize to the person. Tell them you're on a journey to improve your listening skills and ask for their patience while you're working on it. Most people will be grateful that you're trying and will even help you improve your communication skills. Remember, "The art of

effective listening is essential to clear communication, and clear communication is necessary to management success." (J. C. Penney.)[74]

Recently, in an informal interview with Michael Hood[75] (co-founder of VoiceFlow), legendary investor and billionaire Warren Buffett advised, "The one easy way to become worth 50 percent more than you are now—at least—is to hone your communication skills—both written and verbal." An effective leader is an effective communicator. Great communication is the key to successful leadership. I happen to know that Dr. John C. Maxwell spends his time before every talk he does walking through the crowds, talking to people and listening to what they expect to glean from his talk. And then guess what he does? Yep. He adapts his message to their expectations based on what he's heard. No wonder he is such an effective and dynamic speaker. He meets the expected needs of audiences across the world by listening to their wants and needs and desires! Practice reflective listening with everyone, especially if you seem to be in misunderstandings often. Your skill in this area will improve over time if you keep reflecting and listening to their responses. People want to be listened to and understood. Truth be told, you want the same thing. Show them the same courtesy you would want for yourself. To lead the people you are working with, you must know them. To know them, you must listen to them and speak their language as fluently as you speak your own. Remember, "The ear of the leader must ring with the voices of the people." (Woodrow Wilson.)[76]

> "The ear of the leader must ring with the voices of the people."

# CHAPTER 20

# FAKE IT 'TIL YOU MAKE IT

**T**he Effect: If you, as a leader, don't know how to do it, you must pretend that you do. The last thing a leader should show anybody is that they don't know what they're doing.

**The Secret:** If you don't know what you're doing, your people either will figure it out or, chances are, they already know it. Once they know it, if you continue to act like an expert, you're nothing more than a fake. And nobody will follow a fake.

The person who influenced me the most in my stage illusions is a guy named Andre Kole. You may or may not have heard of him but, if you look at the credits at the end of nearly every David Copperfield special, you'll see his name as a magical contributor. Andre is a magical genius. He received an award for being the magical inventor of the decade.

Among the many creations he collaborated with David Copperfield on, the most well-known would be his Statue of Liberty disappearance. Andre, however, did a stage version of this effect where the statue disappeared—from the floor, *up*. That's right: It disappeared starting from the feet, and the head was the last thing to go. At the end of the effect, the statue's head was apparently floating in midair before it disappeared. It was one of the greatest stage illusions ever.

In the early 2000s, I was privileged to do a few of Andre's creations on stage, but far and away the most massive illusion I ever did was

Andre's "Table of Death." This illusion featured twenty-seven 14" solid steel spikes suspended fourteen feet above my head as I was shackled to a table with deadbolt locks. I was given two minutes to get out before the spikes came crashing down on my body. In my version, something went "wrong." There was an explosion, and the spikes fell on me after thirty seconds, only to pass through my body. I stood up, unharmed.

Andre developed this effect years ago. It was featured in 1973 in an episode of *The Magician* starring Bill Bixby called "The Illusion of the Evil Spikes." You can see the clip on YouTube. The magician who "dies" at the beginning is Andre Kole.

Here's the ironic part. When I purchased the illusion from Andre, he told me that when Bill Bixby was doing the illusion in the show, he was in the wrong position. If Andre had not run in and stopped everyone before the spikes fell, the illusion would have actually killed Bill Bixby! Fortunately, it did not. Knowing how an illusion is done and being able to do it are two completely different things.

The number-one question I am asked after every illusion is, "How did you do that?" That's everyone's knee-jerk reaction. I could explain to you in about ten seconds how David Copperfield made the Statue of Liberty disappear (but I won't, so don't ask me!), but that doesn't mean you could actually do it. There is equipment to buy, assistants to train, and a presentation to perfect, which can take multiple years.

I personally believe David Copperfield is the greatest stage magician of our time. But he's not the greatest magician because he knows some secrets; he's the greatest because he's worked and practiced and perfected his presentations and shaped them into moving theatrical pieces that audiences truly care about.

I have seen lots of people imitate David's style and even flat-out copy his presentations. But the best they'll ever be are fakes—cheap imitations of the real person. So I say again: Knowing how to do something doesn't mean you can do the same thing.

Let me clarify it even further. When I see someone starting out in magic, they're so excited that they've learned a secret that they often run out to show their friends way earlier than they should. The results of this are often disastrous, with their friends saying, "That's stupid! I see how that works!" People are swift to spot a fake. Unless you put in the practice and the work, you'll be considered a fake too.

There was a professor at the university I attended who was very popular. He had accomplished many things in his life, and he was barely forty. Some people in his classes were captivated by his stories of meeting legendary people and traveling the world. I always thought there was something about him that didn't quite ring true. Some of my other friends thought the same thing.

One day, we went to our class only to find out he was no longer employed by the university. Yep. He had lied about everything. I don't just mean his stories; he had also lied about having a doctorate in education. He didn't even have a college degree! He had lied his way into a job as a professor at a university! Fake people are almost always exposed.

> **People are swift to spot a fake.**

If a person is fake in one area, almost everyone will assume they're fake in every area. It's a sad truth. The greatest thing we can do is to simply be ourselves. If you look at yourself in the mirror and don't like what you're authentically seeing then you can change—starting today! Here are a few tips about being authentic:

1) **When you've blown it, admit it.** Every one of us makes mistakes. We covered this extensively in chapter 16. The worst thing you can do with an error is to try to cover it up or act as if you didn't do it.

2) **If you've been acting like something you're not, stop it.** Be you. You have a unique contribution to make. Often, this problem comes from somebody comparing themselves to somebody else they perceive to be better than them. Comparison is a very dangerous thing. It leads us down the counterfeit road to hypocrisy. Far too often, we spend money on things we don't need to try to impress people we don't even like. The other thing that causes people to be fake is the fear that if we show others our authentic self, we will not be liked. But let's throw some truth on that with a pointed question: Would you rather be liked for somebody you're truly not or be disliked for who you truly are? If you answered that you'd rather be liked then you have an identity issue and you are dooming yourself to the life of a fraud. Like me or dislike me, at least you'll know the real me. And I'm the best me there is. I'm a lousy copy of anybody else. The same is true of you. Be who you are supposed to be. If you don't like who you are, dedicate yourself for the next sixty days to personal growth. There are lots of books and audio files to listen to that can help you on this journey. You don't have to be fake!

3) **If you've been acting like you know something you don't honestly know or acting as if you're an expert in something you're not, the best thing you can do is admit it.** Chances are, most of the people you think you're fooling already know. If you don't know something, the best thing you can do is be authentic and admit it. Then surround yourself with people who do have the answers or go find the answer. I heard Horst Schultz, former CEO of Ritz-Carlton (famed for its customer service standards), say, "Our employees are never allowed to say, 'I don't know.' That is a lazy response. Instead, they say, 'I don't currently have that answer, but I will find it for you.' That is a proper response." The best response for a leader who doesn't know something is to admit it and then find the answer or find someone with the answer. The worst response is to pretend they know. Your team can sniff out a fake the same way a dog can sniff out fear in a human.

4) **Don't take yourself so seriously.** I know some leaders who can dish it out but who cannot take it. When you act this way, it makes you seem shallow and, yes, fake. Everyone makes mistakes. Everyone blows it. Every public speaker will tell you that, at some point, they blew it on stage. There was some sort of Freudian slip or some word inversion. When the crowd started laughing, the worst thing they could do was pretend it didn't happen. The most human thing they could do was admit it and laugh with the crowd. My dad used to say, "If you can't laugh at yourself, you simply aren't getting the joke." Lighten up! Laugh at your own mistakes. It makes you vulnerable, but it also makes you real and relatable to those your work with.

> The greatest thing we can do is to simply be ourselves.

Let's take a few moments here.

- Write down ways you've been pretending to be something or someone you know you're not.

- Can you admit that to the people you're closest to? If you can't then you may need a new circle of friends who will love you despite your faults.

- Write down what you have learned from each experience of pretending.

- Determine from this point on to be purely authentic. Be real. Be you.

Take a few moments to complete these tasks before you go on. Write all of those down on a separate sheet of paper. When you're done writing them all down, wad the paper up and throw it away.

That may now seem like a waste of time, but it wasn't. There's a huge significance to writing things down, getting them out, and then releasing them. Let throwing the paper away represent you throwing away the "fake" you and keeping the real you!

Frank Abagnale Jr.'s story is an extraordinary one. You may have seen it dramatized in the Steven Spielberg movie *Catch Me If You Can* starring Leonardo DiCaprio. Abagnale spent the first part of his life as a total fraud. And here's the thing: He was really good at it. He assumed at least eight identities, including a US Federal Bureau of Prisons agent, a lawyer, a doctor, and an airline pilot! During this time, he made lots of money by assuming these identities and by passing fraudulent checks all over the world. For a while, he seemed to be living the high life.

Until … he was captured by FBI agent Joseph Shea. After serving some prison time, Abagnale tried to get jobs but was fired from several for lying about his criminal past. He was, however, eventually hired by the FBI as a fraud expert. Knowing the techniques he'd used, he was able to dramatically improve check security in banks. Today, check fraud has been dramatically minimized. One of the first people he was ever honest with was a lady named Kelly. Where he had been dishonest to so many, he determined that he would be completely upfront with her about his past. She accepted him and they are married to this day. One of their sons actually works for the FBI today.

You don't have to impress anybody but yourself. You don't have to be anybody but who you were truly created to be. Be honest. Be authentic. Be you. There are people in this world who need your unique gifts and contributions and who want to meet you. I know— I'm one of them!

> If you can't laugh at yourself, you simply aren't getting the joke."

# CHAPTER 21

# I Cause Change, But I Don't Have to Change

---
**Leadership Illusion # 19**
---

**The Effect:** "I cause change, but I don't have to change."

**The Secret:** A leader who doesn't change but who requires everyone else to change is often seen as a tyrant and a hypocrite. If you want your organization or team to change then you have to model it not only in your organization but in your personal life too.

This illusion is such a double-edged sword. As a leader, you are expected to lead the change in an organization, sometimes against extraordinary resistance. And yet, a leader usually doesn't have a personal problem with the change into which they're leading their team. In fact, they often enjoy being change agents. But when the time comes for the leader to adapt to change themselves, it's a different story.

A 2017 Gallop Poll said that 85 percent of workers worldwide hate their job.[77] That's a staggering statistic. Eighty-five percent of people working hate their job, and yet, they work it. Why? Presumably for money. They're trading their lives for money. They choose security and comfort over the possibility of freedom because their freedom requires risk and change.

If I were to ask that same 85 percent how many of them want their lives and/or jobs to change in the next twelve months, I would venture a guess that nearly 100 percent of them would answer, *"Yes!"* But if I asked that same group, "How many of you would like to personally change?" the responses would go down dramatically. Remember, "For things to change, you have to change." (Jim Rohn.)[78]

> ## 85 percent of workers worldwide hate their job.

Leading people into change that fits our vision is much easier than changing ourselves. We want others to change, but we resist changing ourselves. The hard truth is, if we don't change, change will overtake us. If we, as leaders, don't change then others will not follow us into change either. Asking someone to do something we don't do is the very definition of hypocrisy, and nobody wants to follow a hypocrite.

Jack Welch became the youngest CEO of General Electric at age forty-six. The company was worth $12 billion when he took over and was considered a giant in American industry.[79] When Welch took over GE, he made some sweeping changes. Those changes received immediate widespread criticism from workers and the media.

If there was any product GE was producing that was not ranked number one or two in that industry, he either sold that product off to another company or eliminated the line altogether. Any managers who were in the bottom 10 percent of production were terminated— annually. In 1981, GE had over 400,000 employees. By the end of 1985, GE had under 300,000 employees. Change was the culture of GE during those years. When Jack Welch retired as CEO of General Electric after two decades, the revenues of the company had gone from $25 billion to over $130 billion, with a market capitalization of $400 billion![80]

After he left, GE seemed to neglect the importance of change. Their products began to stagnate, and many of Welch's policies were no longer implemented. As of 2018, their net worth is around $200 billion, less than half.[81]

Change is like a giant wave in the ocean. You can embrace it and ride the wave upward, or you can turn your back on the wave, pretend it isn't coming, resist the change, and inevitably let it overtake you and swallow you up. Remember, "Change before you have to." (Jack Welch.)[82]

General Electric is by no means alone in this category. In the 1990s, lots of people had a PalmPilot personal organizer or a Blackberry mobile device. They were the cutting edge of technology until Steve Jobs and Apple released the iPhone. iPhones were highly criticized because they "didn't even have a keyboard to type things in!" Nor did they "have a roller ball to navigate around." Instead, you just used your finger for everything.

Nobody is having those conversations today. iPhones are now the standard personal digital assistant, and hardly anybody has a Blackberry or PalmPilot anymore.

> **"Change before you have to."**

In fact, the iPhone affected several industries at the same time.

Polaroid cameras were all the rage in the 1980s. GPS devices were popular in the early 2000s. Handheld digital cameras were popular in the 1990s and into the 2000s. Handheld game units were also popular, especially at Christmastime. The iPhone essentially replaced all of these at once.

I could name dozens more:

- **Atari.** Cutting-edge home entertainment system in the 1980s that failed to keep up with the graphical and gaming needs of young consumers who played their games. Instead of creating games, as they had been, they relied on licensing. They were quickly overtaken by Nintendo.

- **Kodak.** Didn't update to digital formatting in time.

- **Blockbuster.** Why rent a video in a store when you can download it online?

- **J. C. Penney.** Didn't market to the consumer and solely relied on its brand name.

- **Commodore Computers.** Wasn't nearly as user-friendly as Apple and refused to update their system. They didn't see the need until it was too late.

- **Radio Shack.** A company that specialized in technology but didn't keep up with the latest technology—how ironic! Online sales killed them.

- **Sony.** Actually had the idea for something similar to the iPod but didn't do it because they were afraid of what it might do to their existing products. The result? Apple *did* do it and took their customers anyway.

- **Pan American World Airways.** They set the standard for airlines until they forgot their customer's number-one need from an airline: safety. They went bankrupt in the early 1990s.

- **MapQuest.** Why print out directions when your phone or car can navigate and read directions out loud for you? Instead of adapting to the wave, the wave swallowed them up.

- **Toys "R" Us.** Never developed an online presence and was put out of business by e-commerce businesses.

- **Sears.** Didn't stay in pace with the digital age, ignored their online presence, and instead relied on customers coming into their stores for sales.

I could go on and on, but you get the point. In another ten to twenty years, some of the best brand-name businesses today will be obsolete for one simple reason: They didn't change.

How do you embrace change so you're not one of the ones swallowed by the wave but are instead one of the great ones surfing the top?

1) **Know that you're going to change.** Whether you like it or not, you're going to change. It's inevitable. It's going to happen. You can either be ahead of the curve or behind it. If you're ahead of it, you can prosper and grow from it. If you're behind it, it can devastate you. But make no mistake: It's coming. A tree that is not growing and changing is dead. The same is true for us. We're either growing or we're dying but, no matter what, we're not staying the same. That is an illusion.

2) **Be proactive, not reactive.** If change is inevitable (which it is), would you rather it be initiated by you or by someone or something else? Of course, this is a rhetorical question. If you are reactive then change will hit you however it chooses to, and you will have to adjust as it comes. Unfortunately, no matter how much one prepares, some changes will be like this. Sudden illness, a car wreck, the unexpected death of a loved one, a financial crisis, a family member in trouble … Life happens. There's no way around it. But, as Jim Rohn once said, "The same wind blows on us all. It's not the blowing of the wind that determines our destination, it's the setting of the sail."[83] All of us face adversity. All of us face change. It's not what happens to us; it's how we deal with what happens to us. That's how we set our sail. When those changes come, we can set our sail and use the wind that was intended to blow our ship crashing into the rocks to instead propel us into our destiny! Set your own course! Remember, "Who won't be ruled by the rudder must be ruled by the rock."[84]

3) **Ask yourself the tough question.** Tough questions can yield transformational answers. Here's a tough one: What

challenges do you see coming into your life in the next six to twelve months that you know you're not resourced or prepared to handle? That question requires brute-force honesty, but that's the beginning of real change. If you choose to ignore those challenges until they're thrust upon you, you'll be operating with a desperate, reactive mindset, and we don't do our best work there. If you decide to be proactive about those decisions now, it can lead you toward a transformation that will make the inevitable changes much easier to handle. A simple example would be a young couple I know who were living in a rented apartment. Their lease was up in six months, and they knew they didn't want to continue living there. They could have chosen to wait six months to address this but, instead, they decided to eliminate some monthly expenses and save that money in a fund. They were going to use the fund to help them move but life happened and one of them had to have an appendectomy. Because they had been proactive in saving money, however, they not only were able to pay their deductible for the surgery, but they also had enough money after six months to rent a home. After another year in that home, using the same methods, they ended up buying the house they were renting for themselves. If we're not proactively looking ahead for upcoming changes, we'll live our lives in damage-control mode, going from one emergency to the next, when some simple planning could have helped us avoid that stressful situation. Being proactive and looking ahead is critical to avoid this lifestyle. Getting in shape doesn't seem nearly as urgent until a person is diagnosed with a disease or has a heart attack. Getting finances in order may not seem as urgent either, until bill collectors start harassing you. Getting key relationships in order may not be a priority until a loved one is gone. Determine today to be proactive in whatever area you need to improve.

Now that you've asked the tough question, there are two more things we need to do.

4)  **Make a list of three things you need to change.** As we've been doing all along, stop now and make your list. Don't go on until you do. Just write three areas in which you know you need change. If you're like me, three was easy. I could have made a list of 100 things I need to change. Again, we're our own worst critic. Let's just deal with three, though. Narrow it down to three big ones. Write down one thing you can do for each one to make a change. Go ahead and embrace it. You're being proactive. You're not waiting for these changes to be thrust upon you. You're doing the work now.

5)  **Change.** I heard Dave Ramsey speak at an event, and he said, "Every person can change. The problem is, they simply don't do it." Yes, you can change. You've made a list. You know what you need to do. Now do it. If you don't, the change will come in a way you either don't expect or don't want. Right now, you can manage it and be somewhat in control of it.

In the 1990s, America Online (AOL) had millions of users on its platform in chatrooms. I know; I was one of them. Everyone looked for a creative email that ended in @aol.com. Then MySpace came along and took a considerable share of those users. Suddenly, they were connected in a different way, sharing photos and other things. It was the top of the industry—until Facebook. The largest share of users now uses Facebook to share their lives with friends (I use that "friend" term loosely, by the way) and families. I suspect that, in the next few years, there will be an entirely different platform that users will embrace and use to connect themselves to each other.

Change is happening around us. Change is happening *to* us. The only question is, will we grab the surfboard of being proactive and jump on top of the tidal wave of change, or will we let that wave sweep over us and toss us wherever it would like?

A leader knows that if they want to stay relevant, they must change. In fact, they must change before their organization will follow them into change.

What changes will you make, starting today? And remember, "Everyone thinks of changing the world, but no one thinks of changing himself." (Leo Tolstoy.)[85]

"Every person can change.
The problem is,
they simply don't do it."

# CHAPTER 22

# Hard Work
# Makes Me a Great Leader

**T**he Effect: "The harder I work, the more successful I will be."

**The Secret:** You can work hard on all the wrong things and still fail miserably. To be effective, you have to spend your time wisely and work smarter, not harder.

Moe was an extremely hard worker. He was a leader of a large group. For the most part, the people he worked with respected him. Like anyone, he had a few naysayers. Truth be told, he had a lot of self-doubts and limiting beliefs too.

There were lots of other people who were more talented and more well-spoken than Moe, but he had been chosen as the leader. When he took over, the group he was leading was in bad shape. They were part of a monstrous corporation that was taking advantage of them. They worked like slaves for little pay and long hours.

Moe stepped up and helped this group believe in themselves and eventually get out from under the hammer of that overbearing organization. Many people seemed more qualified to stand up and give a speech. In fact, when Moe did speak, it elicited some funny remarks because he stuttered. But nobody could argue with Moe's work ethic, and nobody came close to outworking him. So, when the large corporation that Moe's group was working for tried to crush his team's new endeavor, Moe stepped up as the leader and defended them.

The large corporation was Egypt, and "Moe" is better known as "Moses."

Now let me stop here and say that if you're not a person of faith, that's okay. That's not what this is about. This is about leadership, and there's a huge lesson for us here. (If you'd rather skip the rest of this, feel free.)

Moses had experienced some incredible victories in loosening the mighty hand of Egypt from the Israelites and leading them out of slavery. Moses then became a "judge," meaning he would sit in one place and everyone would bring their issues or problems to him, and he would "judge" what was right and wrong between them.

The only problem is that historians estimate that around 2.4 million men, women, and children left Egypt for the Promised Land, and Moses was the only judge. He was working day and night until his father-in-law, Jethro, told him to stop it. He said, "You will weary yourself and everyone else." He then told Moses to learn to delegate to other trustworthy leaders, and that lifted the load.

Notice that Moses's hard work not only wearied him, but it also wearied the people! We can be hard workers and make everyone around us weary and irritated by our lack of leadership. Moses was working hard. There's no doubt about that. But he was definitely not working *smart*. Working smart meant he needed to follow his father-in-law's advice and delegate, which he did, and it all worked out.

Imagine a person who is sent to build a fence around a backyard. That person shows up and works thirteen hours a day for eight weeks. But when the owner, who is paying the bill, looks at the house after eight weeks, there is no fence up. There are pieces laid out, nails set in perfect order, the tools are placed in alphabetical order for ease of locating, and the posts to dig the holes are ready to go.

You, like the owner, would be asking, "What in the world have you been doing for eight weeks?!" Then the person would reply, "I've spent my time organizing all of this. You'll also notice I've painted the fence. It took longer to paint each piece individually, but I figured it would be better to do it that way. I know it took longer, but I didn't have any help."

The owner would then say, "I could have hired three people to come in and finish this job in half the time it took you—and still saved money!"

In this ridiculous example, that person worked hard, but they clearly didn't work *smart*. It's easy to laugh at that but, before we laugh too hard, we have to ask ourselves: Are we doing the same thing?

> Moses was working hard. There's no doubt about that. But he was definitely not working *smart*.

When we willfully work hard at something that is not moving us toward our goal, it is not only not working smart, but (here comes a hard truth) it is also a veiled form of laziness.

Imagine your salary was $525,600 every year. I hear some of you shouting right now! That would be a fantastic salary for most people but, the truth is, if our mindset is messed up, we'll still be broke! We already covered that in chapter 6, "Education Makes Me a Leader." Our income always matches our personal growth.

Here's the thing about successful people and unsuccessful people: They both have exactly the same number of minutes in a year: 525,600 minutes. It's not the amount they have; it's how they spend it that determines their success.

Vilfredo Pareto was a nineteenth-century Italian sociologist who developed what we know today as the Pareto principle. There is a lot of literature that deals in depth with this fascinating principle, but I'm only going to deal with a small portion of it. I'll bet many of you have already heard of the Pareto principle. It's also known as the 80/20 rule.

The rule has many applications, such as 20 percent of the people do 80 percent of the work, or 20 percent of the people own 80 percent of the land (this was his principle applied in his homeland of Italy). However, for our purposes, here is the principle: 20 percent of the people experience 80 percent of the success. Only 20 percent of people do 80 percent of what is necessary to achieve success.

> It's not the amount they have;
> it's how they spend it that
> determines their success.

So, for the purposes of this chapter, the Pareto principle will mean that, if you're willing to do what 80 percent of the people will never do, you can have what only 20 percent of the people will ever have. If you focus on working smarter (doing the 80 percent part that is necessary) then you can be an effective leader. You can be one of the 20 percent who works smarter and not harder.

Here are a few questions related to working smarter:

1) How many hours a week do you work?

2) Are you moving closer to your goals every year, or are you still the same distance away (or even further away)?

**3)** Going back to the goals you wrote out in chapter 6, do your daily activities line up with your written goals?

**4)** What do you need to say "no" to in order to say "yes" to your goals and dreams? Leadership expert John C. Maxwell says, "You must give up to go up."[86] To achieve your goals, you have to give up the *good* to go on to the *great*. What we say "no" to is as important, if not more important, than what we say "yes" to!

**5)** Make a "no" list. Write down the things you're going to give up in order to go up to your goals. Go ahead and do it now. Remember, "Half of the troubles of this life can be traced to saying yes too quickly and not saying no soon enough." (Josh Billings.)[87]

If there was a fire burning in your yard, threatening your house, and you had a water hose on full blast but not pointed at the fire, it wouldn't matter how much time you spent with the hose. For it to be effective, you have to point the hose where it will do the most good.

All of us have the same amount of time in a day, week, month, and year. Determine today to be laser-focused on your goals as a leader. If an opportunity doesn't align with your goals, then say "no"—or, at the very least, "not now"—so you can be focused on what you know you need to be doing.

If you've found yourself working to the point of exhaustion but not getting any closer to your goals, consider pointing the "hose of your goals" at the fire where it will do the most good. Eliminate or delegate what doesn't get you there. That is working smarter!

Remember, "It's only by saying 'No' that you can concentrate on the things that are really important." (Steve Jobs.)[88]

"Half of the troubles of this life
can be traced to saying yes
too quickly and not saying no
soon enough."

# CHAPTER 23

# THE MEASURE OF MY SUCCESS IS HOW MUCH I ACCOMPLISHED

Leadership Illusion #21

**T**he Effect: "The measure of a successful life is how I much I have accomplished and how much I have gained."

**The Secret:** The measure of a truly successful person is how much they pass on and what will live beyond them.

This chapter will be the shortest of all of the chapters, but it is perhaps the most important one. The older I get, the more I think about the topic of *legacy*. I think about what I will pass on to those I love and serve.

The late comedian Jerry Clower shared a story in one of his shows about a billionaire in Texas who passed away. When he died, his will specified that he was to be buried in his gold-plated Cadillac. His body was placed into the driver's seat of the Cadillac and strapped in with a leather seatbelt. As the large crane lowered the Cadillac into the oversized grave, someone in the crowd was overheard saying, "Man! Now that is living!"

That funny story illustrates all too clearly that nothing material is going with us when we leave this earth. As the old saying goes, when a millionaire passed away, someone asked, "How much did he leave?" and the reply came back, "All of it." We take nothing from this world with us. We can, however, leave something of value to others.

We, as humans, tend to cling to our things. We collect stuff that gets passed down to our kids or, more likely, thrown away. We also have a nasty habit of using people and valuing things, when it should be the opposite. We tend to measure success based on how much we accumulate and how expensive the things are that we have collected. I would submit that true success lies in counting the things we have that money cannot buy. It lies in what will live on after we're gone.

There is only one true way our legacies live on, and that is through the people we pour into. One of my favorite quotes from my favorite book reads, "He being dead, still speaks."[89] What we give to others is what will live on after we are gone. That is the essence of *legacy*.

Leaving money to our children and grandchildren is great. It is what wise and responsible people do. But that's not really what this chapter is about. According to a 2015 article, one out of three people have completely spent their inheritance within two years.[90] Just two short years! Don't you want your life's legacy to last longer than two years? If you do, we need to move our focus from money to something more intangible that is more permanent and lasting.

> True success lies in counting the things we have that money cannot buy.

Let's take our last moments in this book to answer this question: What are you focusing on that will live on after you're gone? Knowledge? Wisdom? Family? Faith? All of these intangibles are things that can outlive all of us if we pass them on.

Here are some questions to enlarge our thinking about *legacy*:

1) What are you currently doing that will live on after you are gone?

2) What are some things you are doing that could affect at least two generations after you're gone?

3) Who can you personally mentor and pour yourself into this year?

4) What can you give that will keep on giving after you're gone?

> ## What are you focusing on that will live on after you're gone?

These are the questions that got me thinking beyond myself and into *legacy*. My focus shifted from growing me for the sake of me, to growing me for the sake of growing others. Instead of being a leader positionally, I moved to being a leader who empowers others. Instead of trying to do great things myself, I mentored and empowered others to do great things. Remember, "Carve your name on hearts, not tombstones." (Charles Spurgeon.)[91]

If we shift our thinking from what we have and what we can acquire to what we can give and enable others to do, we will have made a monumental move toward the highest level of leadership: empowering others to live their dreams and destinies!

Think of it this way: If you had $10 billion, would you want to leave that as an inheritance to your children, grandchildren, or other loved ones, or would you rather bury all of it with you in the ground, never to be seen or used again? I hope you answered that you would want to give it away to be used after you're gone.

Here's the truth: The knowledge and experience you have are worth far more than money! What you don't pass on before you die will be buried with you. That's why we must pour into others, especially those we love and care about, so that our knowledge and experience will be passed on to our loved ones. If we don't pass it on then all of our personal growth will be for nothing. If we do pass it on, they will stand on our shoulders and use our knowledge and experience to do even greater things. That is the essence of a *legacy*!

A month ago, I was typing this book while sitting beside the Dead Sea in Israel. At 1,388 feet below sea level, the Dead Sea is the lowest point on Earth. It's fun to go out and float in the water, which is so dense that you cannot sink. The mud and water have healing properties for those with skin conditions.

At 33 percent salinity, it is also the saltiest body of water in the world. Because of this (and a few other reasons), the Dead Sea is appropriately named. Nothing can survive in the water. There are no fish or small organisms. There are warning signs posted all over about drinking the water. If you were to drink a few ounces of the water from the Dead Sea, it could kill you.

Although you can float on top of the water, you cannot drink it. The Dead Sea is dead. Why? Because it is the lowest land point on Earth, and it does nothing but take in. There is no outlet from the sea (it's actually a large lake or a reservoir) to any other point. It takes in and takes in, but never gives out. That is a recipe for death.

The same is true for us. If all we do with the knowledge, wisdom, and other things we've been given is keep them to ourselves, those things die with us.

Instead of being a reservoir like the Dead Sea, we need to be rivers. Water passes through rivers. It keeps providing life for those downstream. As leaders, our goal should be to provide life, empowerment, and legacy to those serving with us. The true measure of our success is not merely what we do; it is what we give to others that lives on beyond us. Remember, "Legacy is not leaving something for people. It's leaving something in people." (Peter Strople.)[92]

Instead of being a reservoir
we need to be rivers.

# CONCLUSION

Congratulations on taking the entire journey! We've covered our twenty-one leadership Illusions. There are more that we could have included. I'm sure you've even thought as you read this, *Why hasn't he mentioned _____?!* We'll leave that conversation open for a future time.

I know you are an incredible person simply because you've made it this far. Most people who start reading a book don't actually finish it![93] You're already in that impressive minority.

I'm going to give you all twenty-one again, but instead of listing the illusions, I'm going to list the secrets (truths):

1) Nobody is a born leader. Leadership is an acquired knowledge that any serious student can learn.

2) Your title doesn't entitle you to anything. Leadership is influence, and a title doesn't give you that. Influence is gained by adding value to those you serve with.

3) Personal growth is more important than our initial education. People don't follow diplomas. Self-education and personal growth are far more important than a diploma.

4) Talent doesn't entitle you to leadership. It's not how much talent you have; it's how much you use those talents to empower and add value to others.

5) Nobody gets there alone. You need a great team around you in order to succeed. That team should fill in each other's weaknesses and operate using their natural strengths.

6) You alone are responsible. Whether you succeed or fail, you must take responsibility for your own actions, as well as the actions of your team. Your success is directly related to you taking ownership of your life.

7) What you ignore will bite you—hard. Nobody has ever moved forward by ignoring problems. Nobody has ever grown by waiting around for something to happen. It takes an intentional plan of growth and success to get to where you need to be.

8) Procrastination kills. What you put off to tomorrow often never gets done. Prioritize and put immediate action into that plan.

9) Doing everything yourself and believing that nobody can do it better than you kills teams. Don't do things for your team. Empower them to do it. Give them the freedom to fail and learn and grow. That's how dynamic teams are built. Don't be a manager who controls—be a leader who empowers!

10) Acknowledging that you don't know everything makes you wise. Don't ask "how" you can know something. Ask, "Who do I know who knows how to do this?"

11) Nothing great in life is gained without risk. Playing it safe all of the time is a short road to mediocrity. If you want to succeed, you have to take calculated (not foolish) risks.

12) Small details can sink large ships. If you're not a detail-oriented person, get a team around you filled with detail-oriented people. Those details can make or break you.

13) Even if you've blown it, you can still be a leader. Mistakes are our best friends in life—if we learn from them. Acknowledge your mistakes, learn from them, and then go on. You can be a more effective leader if you do this.

14) Treating everyone the same way is one of the most insensitive things we can do as leaders. Everyone is different. Everyone has a different communication style. It's our job as leaders to learn how our teams communicate, understand their temperaments, and then speak their language according to their needs.

15) Criticism can help you grow. Shake off personal attacks, but don't dismiss criticism so quickly. There are truths in there that, if applied, can help us grow into better leaders.

16) Confidence is an essential element of a leader. Confidence is a trust in the abilities you've been given to help and empower others. Make it about others, not yourself.

17) Communication will make or break you as a leader. Don't assume everyone knows. Use reflective listening techniques to ensure accurate communication is happening.

18) Nobody follows a fake. No matter where you are in your personal growth journey, be a real, authentic leader. Be honest.

19) If you don't personally change, you will not make it. Change is inevitable. You can either change yourself or be forced to change in a way you probably won't enjoy.

20) Work smarter, not harder. It's not the number of hours you put in; it's how your time is focused and how you use it to further your life goals.

21) The true measure of success is in what you pass on to others. *Legacy* is about giving something intangible to your children's children, as well as to those you influence and empower today.

Now that we've completed the book, what's next? I would encourage you to find three of these illusions you know you've been guilty of and take corrective steps. Look over the notes you made for the questions and take the action steps.

When I was a child and first learning about magic, I saw a magician perform a trick with a rope. He fooled me over and over again. Knowing I had a genuine interest in performing (and not merely knowing the secret), he graciously showed me how it was done. Once I saw exactly how it worked, I couldn't unsee it. In fact, it was permanently burned into my mind. I ended up using that effect in my professional magic shows for the next thirty years and have fooled hundreds of thousands of people with it. The difference between me and those audiences is that I know the truth of how the effect is done and they don't. If they knew the truth, they would not only not be fooled any longer, but they'd never see the illusion again.

That's how truth is for each one of us. As the Bible verse says, "You shall know the truth, and the truth shall set you free." (John 8:32.) Truth puts each one of us in a place where it is undeniable. I can tell you the sky is green, but a short walk outside and a glance upward will show you the truth, and my words will be meaningless afterward.

> If they knew the truth they'd never see the illusion again.

You've been given some powerful truths in this book. These are truths that, now that you've seen them, cannot be denied. Perhaps you already knew most of them. I hope you had at least a few *aha!* moments like I did with that magician years ago. In the words of Witold Gombrowicz, "Do you want to know who you are? Don't ask. Act! Action will delineate and define you."[94]

As I said earlier, there is a vast difference between knowing how something is done and being able to actually do it. You've now been armed with knowledge. You know how these illusions work. You know the next steps to take to grow. But all of that is meaningless if you don't actually apply the truths you've learned! No farmer has ever grown a field of crops by talking about it. They had to sow, cultivate, and harvest.

An unopened present doesn't bless anybody. An unsung song doesn't move anybody. An uneaten meal doesn't satisfy anybody. A well-planned workout that never happens doesn't change anybody. If what is prepared isn't turned into action, it's all meaningless information. I want these truths to mean something for you, and that requires action on your part. Remember, "An idea not coupled with action will never get any bigger than the brain cell it occupied." (Arnold Glasow.)[95]

> "Do you want to know who you are? Don't ask. Act! Action will delineate and define you."

You now know the truth. Apply it to your life and it will not only change your life, but also the lives of those you influence and lead. Tony Robbins said, "The path to success is to take massive, determined action."[96] Benjamin Franklin said, "Well done is better than well said."[97]

We're done talking. *Now* is the time to *do it!* Apply these truths and you're going to see a significant life change, especially in your leadership skills. Take small steps at first, then graduate up to massive action! You can do it!

You'll have an incredible story to tell on the other side of this, and I can't wait to hear it!

"Well done is better than
well said."

# SPECIAL THANKS

- To my family for your continued love and support in this journey.
- To my mother and father. Your belief in me in word and deed has made all the difference in my life.
- To my church family, and especially Dr. Ronnie Phillips, Jr. for your prayers and support.
- To the mentors who have modeled true leadership for me: Dr. Kenneth Hartley, Sr., Dr. Jim Whitmire, Dr. Ron Phillips, Dr. John C. Maxwell, and Governor Mike Huckabee. You have lived out all of the principles in this book right in front of my eyes.
- To Brandon Lunsford, Jay Craig, and Bill Marion. True friends show up when others walk out. You are true friends.
- To my lifelong friend, Captain Richard C. McDaniel, USN. You have achieved massive influence and have modeled leadership in so many ways. I am so blessed to call you my friend and to learn from you.
- To Robben Mathews for showing me the power of belief, forgiveness, restoration, and elevating others above yourself.
- To Chris and Melissa Rollins for helping me understand who I truly am as well as others around me.
- To Tom Telesco for believing in me and coaching me to write this.
- To Delatorro McNeal, II for pushing me to my full potential and lighting the pathway to my destiny with fire.
- To Gary Arblaster for being a friend who sticks closer than a brother.

- To Al Denson for giving of your wisdom and resources to lift others up. You model servant leadership in your everyday life.

- To David Huckabee for letting me know it's perfectly fine and necessary to laugh often and laugh loudly. Thanks, friend.

- And most of all, to my Lord and Savior, Jesus Christ. You gave the greatest leadership speech ever in just two words, "Follow me." Thank you for grace, love, forgiveness, and salvation.

# ABOUT THE AUTHOR

**Ken Hartley**

Ken Hartley is an inspirational keynote speaker, an accomplished singer, a talented illusionist, a skilled actor, a bestselling author, a gifted teacher, and a transformation agent. He has been a singer and actor on stage and screen since he was five years old. He has also performed as a professional illusionist all over the world, has authored several books, and has released two solo CDs. He is a Certified Speaker, Trainer, and Coach with The John Maxwell Team as well as an Advanced Certified Human Behavior Consultant with Personality Insights and Dr. Robert Rohm.

As an inspirational speaker, he has shared the stage with speakers like Rudy Guiliani, Colin Powell, James Smith, Delatorro McNeal, II, Zig Ziglar, Mike Huckabee, and Dr. John C. Maxwell. His skills have also been featured on television networks like Fox, ABC, NBC, CBS, TBN, Daystar, and INSP. He loves to encourage and challenge people to overcome limiting obstacles and step into their God-given destinies. He is considered by his peers and clients to be a master speaker and communication expert. His presentations are often described as entertaining, engaging, and transformational.

Ken has over 30 years of fulltime experience in various megachurches across the United States and brings those skills, plus his training in leadership and communication, to organizations as a transformation agent to effect change and help individuals and organizations grow into who they are supposed to be.

He lives in Chattanooga, TN with his wife, four children, and one grandchild.

To Contact Ken Hartley
please email:
ken@hartleyleadership.com
or visit:
www.hartleyleadership.com

# NOTES

_____

_____

_____

_____

_____

_____

_____

_____

_____

_____

_____

_____

_____

_____

_____

# ENDNOTES

[1] Gallup Poll- Congress and the Public-
https://news.gallup.com/poll/1600/congress-public.aspx

[2] Proverbs 29:18.

[3] This quote has been attributed to 20th century Philospher Elbert
Hubbard as well as a 20th century magician, Karl Germain. It appears in
both of their writings and it is unclear who said it first.

[4] Nipperdey, *Deutsche Geschichte 1866-1918. vol. 2: Machtstaat vor der
Demokratie* (1992) p 421, translated in Richard J. Evans, *Rereading
German History: From Unification to Reunification, 1800-1996* (1997)
p39

[5] Google "influence definition." I thought it was well done. Webster's
Dictionary defines "influence" as "the power or capacity of causing an
effect in indirect or intangible ways."

[6] Dr. John C. Maxwell, "The Law of Influence." *The 21 Irrefutable Laws of
Leadership.* p11.

[7] From the cover of the program of the memorial service for Calvin
Coolidge in 1933.

[8] Jim Rohn, "Building Your Network Marketing Business," audio program,
2006.

[9] https://www.benzinga.com/media/18/10/12558948/out-of-luck-lottery-
winners-who-have-gone-bankrupt

[10] Dean Graziosi, Tony Robbins, "Come Discover The KBB Method &
Tap Into A $355 Million Dollar a Day Industry" Webinar, April 30, 2019.

[11] https://www.nba.com/thunder/team/kevin_durant.html

[12] Muhammad Ali Quotes. BrainyQuote.com, BrainyMedia Inc, 2019.
https://www.brainyquote.com/quotes/muhammad_ali_145945, accessed
May 22, 2019.

[13] From the cover of the program of the memorial service for Calvin
Coolidge in 1933.

[14] https://www.johnmaxwell.com/blog/one-is-too-small-a-number/, May
31, 2011.

[15] To find out more about Maria Cristina's work or to donate, go to
http://mariacristinafoundation.org/

[16] John C. Maxwell Quotes. BrainyQuote.com, BrainyMedia Inc, 2019.
https://www.brainyquote.com/quotes/john_c_maxwell_383606, accessed
May 23, 2019.

[17] Marie Curie, Pierre Curie (1923), as translated by Charlotte Kellogg and Vernon Lyman Kellogg, p. 168.

[18] Jim Rohn, "Building Your Network Marketing Business" audio program, 2006

[19] Michael Ammar, "Michael Ammar Live at the Magic Castle" video, 1990

[20] *Osborne, Tim (1937). Introduction to Cups and Balls Magic.*

[21] http://www.romeshg.com/writers-procrastination-routines

[22] **Hugo, 1831/1978; Wallace & Pear, 1977, p. 7, quoted in J. Sturrock's Introduction.**

[23] https://www.cmuse.org/mozart-midnight-masterpiece-don-giovanni-overture/

[24] https://www.cbsnews.com/news/the-whys-and-why-nows-of-procrastination/

[25] https://www.azquotes.com/quote/543484

[26] https://www.azquotes.com/quote/543463

[27] https://johnsonsearchgroup.com/2017/01/yesterdays-home-runs-not-win-todays-game/

[28] https://quotesonfinance.com/quote/79/albert-einstein-compound-interest

[29] http://www.getmotivation.com/motivationblog/2010/10/the-seven-cs-of-success-by-chris-widener/

[30] Durant, Will, 1885-1981. *The Story of Philosophy : The Lives and Opinions of the Great Philosophers of the Western World.* New York :Simon and Schuster, 1961, p87.

[31] Norman Vincent Peale Quotes. BrainyQuote.com, BrainyMedia Inc, 2019.
https://www.brainyquote.com/quotes/norman_vincent_peale_159730, accessed May 23, 2019.

[32] https://www.truman.edu/about/history/our-namesake/truman-quotes/

[33] Jim Rohn, Weekend Seminar Audio 1999.

[34] https://www.bostoncontemporaries.com/2017/12/05/quote-day-dale-carnegie-2/

[35] https://succeedfeed.com/peter-drucker-quotes/, #5

[36] https://beleaderly.com/leaderly-quote-managers-light-a-fire-under-people/

[37] Henry Ford Quotes. BrainyQuote.com, BrainyMedia Inc, 2019.
https://www.brainyquote.com/quotes/henry_ford_151861, accessed May 23, 2019.

[38] https://beleaderly.com/emerging-leader-spotlight-maria-shi/

[39] https://www.cbsnews.com/news/ronald-reagan-remembered/

[40] "A Time for Choosing" speech, Ronald Reagan, October 27,1964, Los Angeles, California.

[41] [FSG]1897, [1863 September 21: Date on Diary Entry], Notes from a Diary 1851-1872 Volume I by Sir Mountstuart E. Grant Duff, Page 237, John Murray, London.

[42] Theodore Roosevelt Quotes. BrainyQuote.com, BrainyMedia Inc, 2019. https://www.brainyquote.com/quotes/theodore_roosevelt_120663, accessed May 23, 2019.

[43] Rudy, 1993, Bonus Features, *Rudy, the Real Story.*

[44] https://www.golfdigest.com/story/yogi-berra-1995-2015-famously-said-90-percent-of-putts-that-are-short-dont-go-in

[45] Bible, Hebrews 11:1.

[46] https://www.inc.com/glenn-leibowitz/20-inspiring-quotes-to-help-you-rise-above-failure-fulfill-your-dreams.html

[47] https://www.thewoodeneffect.com/words-of-wisdom/

[48] Maxwell, John C. *Leadership Gold*, Thomas Nelson Publishing, 2008, Chapter 17.

[49] https://www.uky.edu/~eushe2/Pajares/OnFailingG.html

[50] https://www.uky.edu/~eushe2/Pajares/OnFailingG.html

[51] https://www.visitmacysusa.com/article/history-macys-humble-beginnings-stunning-success

[52] https://www.biography.com/political-figure/winston-churchill

[53] http://www.baberuth.com/quotes/

[54] Bible account about these events in Simon Peter's life is found in Matthew 26:31-35, 69-74; Acts 2:14-41.

[55] https://www.inc.com/benjamin-p-hardy/23-michael-jordan-quotes-that-will-immediately-boost-your-confidence.html

[56] http://www.vincelombardi.com/quotes.html

[57] I would highly recommend *Positive Personality Profiles, published in 1993* by Dr. Robert Rohm if you want to learn more about DISC. Their website is https://www.personality-insights.com/

[58] International Maxwell Certification Mentorship Session, Orlando, Florida, February 20, 2018.

[59] https://beleaderly.com/leaderly-quote-look-for-people-whose-skills-are-the-opposite-of-yours/

[60] Jim Rohn, Weekend Seminar Audio 1999.

[61] www.ziglar.com

[62] https://www.theguardian.com/books/2015/mar/24/jk-rowling-tells-fans-twitter-loads-rejections-before-harry-potter-success

[63] https://www.entrepreneur.com/article/197542

[64] https://www.glennbeck.com/2017/12/22/how-george-lucas-overcame-rejection-and-made-star-wars-one-of-the-best-movie-franchises-in-history/

[65] https://www.jackcanfield.com/blog/write-a-book/

[66] 1898, Little Journeys to the Homes of American Statesmen by Elbert Hubbard, Section: William H. Seward, Start Page 363, Quote Page 370, G. P. Putnam's Sons, New York; The Knickerbocker Press, New York. (Edition copyright 1898; Reprint date November 1901).

[67] President Theodore Roosevelt's speech, *Citizenship in the Republic*, April 23, 1910, at the University of Paris.

[68] Anne Frank Quotes. BrainyQuote.com, BrainyMedia Inc, 2019. https://www.brainyquote.com/quotes/anne_frank_379577, accessed May 23, 2019.

[69] Quote from Charles Dickens's New Christmas Story: Dr. Marigold's Prescriptions, 1865

[70] https://www.usatoday.com/story/opinion/2018/12/03/george-hw-bush-neil-bush-points-light-service-volunteer-column/2183960002/

[71] Ziglar.com

[72] While some have attributed this quote to Winston Churchill, biographer Richard Langworth claims that is erroneous. I was unable to find who actually said this, but it is a great quote.

[73] Mehrabian, Albert, *Silent Messages: Implicit Communication of Emotions and Attitudes,* Wadsworth Publishing Company Inc., Belmont, California, 1971.

[74] James Cash Penney Quotes. BrainyQuote.com, BrainyMedia Inc, 2019. https://www.brainyquote.com/quotes/james_cash_penney_226548, accessed May 23, 2019.

[75] https://www.cnbc.com/2018/12/05/warren-buffett-how-to-increase-your-worth-by-50-percent.html

[76] "The Leaders of Men", speech at the University of Tennessee (17 June 1890), in *The Politics of Woodrow Wilson*, p. 74.

[77] https://news.gallup.com/opinion/chairman/212045/world-broken-workplace.aspx

[78] Jim Rohn, Weekend Seminar Audio 1999.

[79] https://www.antiessays.com/free-essays/Jack-Welch-Manager-Of-The-583801.html

[80] https://www.cnbc.com/2017/11/17/former-ge-ceo-jack-welch-how-to-be-a-great-leader.html

[81] https://www.cnbc.com/2018/02/28/ken-langone-ge-destruction-happened-after-jack-welch-left-as-ceo.html

[82] https://www.ncbi.nlm.nih.gov/pubmed/22710206

[83] Jim Rohn, Weekend Seminar Audio 1999.

[84] G. Torriano Italian Proverbs 286. Simpson and Speake, *The Oxford Dictionary of Proverbs*, Oxford University Press, 2009.

[85] https://quotes.yourdictionary.com/author/leo-tolstoy/613755#t_change

[86] Maxwell, John C. "The Law of Sacrifice," *The 21 Irrefutable Laws of Leadership.*

[87] https://www.forbes.com/sites/sap/2015/08/12/quotes-on-saying-no/#1a3064975555

[88] Interview with Business Week, 2004.

[89] Bible, Hebrews 11:4.

[90] https://www.marketwatch.com/story/one-in-three-americans-who-get-an-inheritance-blow-it-2015-09-03

[91] Smagorinsky & Taxel, *The Discourse of Character Education*, Taylor & Francis, 2005.

[92] Peter Strople's Twitter, August 23, 2018, 9:48 a.m.

[93] https://www.theifod.com/how-many-people-finish-books/

[94] Gombrowicz, Witold, 1988: *Diary, Vol. II* (Chicago; Northwestern University Press, 1988), 130.

[95] https://www.quotes.net/quote/59183

[96] Robbins, Anthony, *Awaken the Giant Within.*

[97] Franklin, Benjamin, *Poor Richard's Almanack.*